2004 05 27

Developing Emotional Intelligence

A Guide to Behavior Management and Conflict
Resolution in Schools

Richard J. Bodine
Donna K. Crawford

Research Press • 2612 North Mattis Avenue • Champaign, Illinois 61822
www.researchpress.com

Cover design by Publication Services, Inc.
Composition by Publication Services, Inc.
Printed by McNaughton & Gunn
ISBN 0–87822–421–1
Library of Congress Catalog Number 99-73651

Contents

Tables   *vii*
Preface   *ix*

INTRODUCTION
Developing Emotional Intelligence through Behavior
Management and Conflict Resolution Education   *1*

CHAPTER 1
Our Collective Emotional Crisis   *11*
    Responsible versus compliant behavior   14
    Learning transfer   15
    Today's behavioral scene   17
    The role of schools   26
    Emotional crisis   28

CHAPTER 2
Emotional Intelligence   *33*
    What is emotional intelligence?   34
        Knowing one's emotions   35
        Managing emotions   37
        Motivating oneself   39
        Recognizing emotions in others   43
        Handling relationships   44
    Developing emotional intelligence   45

CHAPTER 3
Classroom Barriers to Emotional Development   *51*
    The peaceable classroom   53
    Punishments and rewards   57
    Systems change   61

CHAPTER 4

A Psychological Framework for Managing the Classroom for Emotional Intelligence   65
How and why people behave   70
Basic psychological needs and internal motivation   71
Quality world   73
Total behavior   74
Reality therapy   76
Counseling environment   77
Procedures that lead to change   78

CHAPTER 5

A Management System for Creating Responsible Learners and Citizens   81
A process, not a recipe   81
Teachable behaviors and facilitative probes   82
Essential system contexts   90
Building community: A cooperative context   91
Managing behavior without coercion   94
Punishment or discipline   96
Sense-based behavior management systems   100
Rights and responsibilities   102

CHAPTER 6

How to Manage the Classroom for Emotional Intelligence   111
Responsibility education   112
Rules for rules   114
Class meetings   118
Life rules   121
C.A.R.E. time   126
Time-out   131
Verbal plan   133
Written plan   133
Guidelines for C.A.R.E. time and time-out   147

CHAPTER 7
*Extending Emotional Intelligence through Conflict
Resolution Education   149*
Perceptions of peace   150
Peacemaking behavior   151
Practices for managing conflict in schools   153
Conflict resolution   154
Perceptions of conflict   156
Origins of conflict   158
Limited resources   158
Different values   159
Responses to conflict   160
Soft responses   161
Hard responses   161
Principled responses   162
Outcomes of different responses   162
Principles of conflict resolution   165
Separate people from the problem   165
Focus on interests, not positions   167
Invent options for mutual gain   168
Use objective criteria   169
Foundation abilities for conflict resolution   170
Orientation abilities   170
Perception abilities   171
Emotion abililities   171
Communication abilities   172
Creative thinking abilities   172
Critical thinking abilities   173
Conflict resolution problem-solving processes   174
Conflict resolution problem-solving strategies   175

APPENDIX
*Facilitating Emotional Intelligence: Activities for
Developing Teachable Abilities   179*
Activity 1: Basic Needs   181
Activity 2: Basic Needs and Conflict   187

Activity 3: Limited Resources Conflicts and Basic
        Needs   193
Activity 4: Different Values Conflicts and Basic
        Needs   196
Activity 5: Rights and Responsibilities   201
Activity 6: Responsible Behavior and Basic Needs   206
Activity 7: Basic Needs and the Social Context   209
Discussion Topics for Class Meetings   212

About the Authors   215

Tables

5.1 Total Behavior of Learners under Different Management Styles 95

5.2 Choices for Learners under Different Management Styles 97

5.3 Punishment versus Discipline 98

5.4 Characteristics of Sense-Based versus Rule-Abundant Behavior Management Systems 103

5.5 Rights and Responsibilities 105

5.6 Leal Rights and Responsibilities 106

6.1 Life Rules Translated into Classroom Behaviors 123

6.2 Normal Classroom Strategies versus Responses with Unresponsive/Defiant Students 135

6.3 Sample Interchanges between Teacher and Unresponsive/Defiant Student 136

7.1 Peacemaker versus Peacebreaker Behaviors 151

7.2 Prevalent Practices versus Conflict Resolution 154

7.3 Conflict Myths and Conflict Realities 164

Preface

As career educators, we have consistently advocated for quality learning and cooperative endeavor, believing the two notions are inextricably linked. It has been our good fortune to have the opportunity to formulate innovative educational practices and to try out and refine our ideas in public school settings. It has also been our rare privilege to collaborate with our colleagues to create a number of pragmatic publications that have been well utilized by the educational community.

With our friend Fred Schrumpf, we collaborated on *Peer Mediation: Conflict Resolution in Schools*, a training and implementation guide for establishing a peer mediation program in middle and high schools.[1] It was in this publication that we introduced the idea of basic psychological needs as the origin of conflict. Based on our new learning, gained from 5 years of using the original version of *Peer Mediation* to train numerous adults and young people in mediation, we significantly revised this publication in 1997.[2]

The concept of "rights and responsibilities" presented in chapter 5 as the underlayment of a behavior management plan was conceived by Bodine and first used as the basis for a schoolwide responsibility education and behavior management plan in 1973. "Rights and responsibilities" first appeared in our publication *The School for Quality Learning: Managing the School and Classroom the Deming Way*, which we coauthored with Robert G. Hoglund.[3] In this book we proposed fundamental changes to the educational system to provide need-fulfilling instructional experiences for all learners—regardless of race, gender, or socioeconomic status. An important management style transformation advanced in this publication centered on a schoolwide discipline and responsibility education program and classroom management practices consistent with the school consensus on rights and responsibilities, and on the few behaviors targeted to be extinguished. This transformation included the use of reality therapy as a prime management tool, using the concept of "life rules" for the classroom and the intervention strategies of C.A.R.E. time and time-out.

In *Creating the Peaceable School: A Comprehensive Program for Teaching Conflict Resolution*, another collaboration with Fred Schrumpf, we provided a vision of peace and a workable plan for achieving that vision in our schools.[4] We built upon the fundamentals of peer mediation, adding the strategies of negotiation and group problem solving. In this publication, we first advanced the notion of "sense-based" behavior expectations and exhorted the necessity to manage behavior without coercion. This training program was designed to extend the benefits of conflict resolution training to all members of the school environment, as opposed to only a few peer mediators, and to construct an environment in which conflict resolution processes would become "the way we do things here." This training also extended conflict resolution education to elementary as well as secondary schools.

In our publications *Conflict Resolution Education: A Guide to Implementing Programs in Schools, Youth-Serving Organizations, and Community and Juvenile Justice Settings*[5] and *The Handbook of Conflict Resolution Education: A Guide to Building Quality Programs in Schools*,[6] we provided a comprehensive discourse on youth-focused conflict resolution education. In these publications, we first delineated the foundational abilities of conflict resolution and argued that programs must address these as well as provide problem-solving processes.

With the writing of each of these volumes, our ideas have coalesced. Some of what we have to say in the present volume we have said before in these previous publications. We reprise our thoughts on how control theory, reality therapy, rights and responsibilities, and conflict resolution will help us achieve schools where true learning can occur. But in this volume, we reconstruct these ideas and present them in a new light—that is, in the context of what we now know about emotional intelligence. Basically, no conflict resolution or responsibility education program—and no behavior management program—will be successful unless learners and educators alike recognize the importance of emotions and learn to use them intelligently. A clear mission exists to teach and foster the abilities of emotional intelligence in our schools. Without doing that, schools will not realize their ultimate purpose of producing responsible future citizens.

This book makes the case that schools must pay attention to the development of emotional competencies in our future citizens. The management of behavior in schools is a crucial activity to create a climate conducive to learning. However, practices that constitute that management often are compliance driven and actually detrimental to emotional development. It is possible to manage behavior, thus creating a productive learning climate but also facilitating emotional development and responsible behavior.

- The introduction of this book details the relationship between behavior management and emotional intelligence and advances the notion that the marriage of the two is required to realize the vision of the peaceable school.

- Chapter 1 argues that youth and the world in which they live have changed dramatically and the ability to respond intelligently and productively to that world requires more than behavioral compliance to externally imposed standards.

- Chapter 2 explains the elements that comprise emotional intelligence and contrasts what is often typical behavior with emotionally intelligent behavior.

- Chapter 3 presents the case that just doing a better job at our present endeavors in schools will likely have little effect. Accomplishing the mission of developing future responsible citizens for our democratic society requires system change to align practice with intent.

- Chapter 4 explains behavior from the psychology of control theory and argues that such a view of internal motivation is necessary for individual behavioral self-evaluation. Reality therapy is presented as management behaviors that create an environment supportive of behavioral examination and change, and as an intervention strategy to encourage and create expectations for behavioral self-evaluation.

- Chapter 5 outlines emotional intelligence as abilities that can be developed through facilitation within a systems environment that allows for and demands behavioral self-evaluation. The basic framework of a systemwide behavior management plan to foster the development of emotional intelligence is described.

- Chapter 6 introduces management tools for noncoercive behavioral interventions, with emphasis on questioning techniques to focus individuals on present behavior, on behavioral goals, and on the extent to which the present behavior is or can be need- or goal-fulfilling. Responsibility is defined as acquiring personal need satisfaction without denying need satisfaction to all others in a social context.

- Chapter 7 depicts conflict resolution education as providing important tools that enable individuals in disputes to craft plans for future constructive, or at least not destructive, relationships. Because of the omnipresent nature of conflict, the ability to use these tools is important in enabling an individual to take effective control of his or her life. Our publication *Creating the Peaceable School: A Comprehensive Program for Teaching Conflict Resolution* is a training program to provide youth with these tools.

- The appendix presents seven activities to give learners a basic understanding of their behavior based on control theory. Adapted from *Creating the Peaceable School: A Comprehensive Program for Teaching Conflict Resolution* and the revised edition of *Peer Mediation: Conflict Resolution in Schools*, these activities emphasize the notion that all behavior is purposeful and chosen in order to facilitate an understanding of the relationship between rights and responsibilities and to promote awareness that behaviors that may be need fulfilling for the individual can be problematic in a social context such as school. Class meeting discussion topics are suggested to reinforce and extend understanding of the concepts covered in the lessons.

Endnotes

1. F. Schrumpf, D. K. Crawford, and H. C. Usadel, *Peer Mediation: Conflict Resolution in Schools* (Champaign, IL: Research Press, 1991).

2. F. Schrumpf, D. K. Crawford, and R. J. Bodine, *Peer Mediation: Conflict Resolution in Schools,* rev. ed. (Champaign, IL: Research Press, 1997).

3. D. K. Crawford, R. J. Bodine, and R. G. Hoglund, *The School for Quality Learning: Managing the School and Classroom the Deming Way* (Champaign, IL: Research Press, 1993).

4. R. J. Bodine, D. K. Crawford, and F. Schrumpf, *Creating the Peaceable School: A Comprehensive Program for Teaching Conflict Resolution* (Champaign, IL: Research Press, 1994).

5. D. K. Crawford and R. J. Bodine, *Conflict Resolution Education: A Guide to Implementing Programs in Schools, Youth-Serving Organizations, and Community and Juvenile Justice Settings* (Washington, DC: U. S. Department of Justice and U. S. Department of Education, 1996).

6. R. J. Bodine and D. K. Crawford, *The Handbook of Conflict Resolution Education: A Guide to Building Quality Programs in Schools* (San Francisco: Jossey-Bass, 1998).

Developing Emotional Intelligence through Behavior Management and Conflict Resolution Education

Emotional intelligence is the intelligent use of emotions: You intentionally make your emotions work for you by using them to guide your behavior and thinking in ways that enhance your results.[1] Your emotions give you valuable information about yourself, about other people, and about situations. Being aware of your feelings and behavior as well as others' perceptions of you can influence your actions in such a way that they work to your benefit.

Daniel Goleman, in his book *Emotional Intelligence*,[2] tells of a massive survey of parents and teachers that shows a worldwide trend for the present generation of children to be more troubled emotionally than the last: more lonely and depressed, more angry and unruly, more nervous and prone to worry, more impulsive and aggressive. He maintains that the remedy lies in how we prepare our young people for life and that at present we leave the emotional education of our children to chance. He foresees a day when education will routinely include inculcating essential human competencies such as self-awareness, self-control, and empathy, as well as the arts of listening, resolving conflicts, and cooperation. It is becoming increasingly clear that the day is here for our educational institutions to address the development of emotional competence in all young people. This book is about doing that in our classrooms and our schools.

The purpose of this book is to delineate ways to create a behavior management program that promotes and supports the development of emotional intelligence. The case will be made that doing so clearly calls for a shift in discipline strategies away from control and compliance, based largely on punishment and external rewards, toward a program of education for developing responsible citizens. The purpose of such a school behavior management program is to assist all persons in becoming more effective managers of their own behavior by learning to make responsible, need-fulfilling choices that result in constructive, successful behaviors. The role of the behavior manager is to develop capacity in each student, not simply to judge the present ability of each to meet societal behavioral norms. This is a call to educate rather than to control.

The case will also be made that the shift we ask managers—school level and classroom level—to consider in no way suggests that these managers should abandon the behavior management of students. Behavior management is necessary to establish a social order that allows masses of students and adults to associate productively in the school environment. Does the responsibility for constructive behavior rest only with adults? May students shoulder some of it?

Sylwester points out that

> we know emotion is very important to the educative
> process because it drives attention, which drives learning
> and memory. We've never really understood emotion,
> however, and so don't know how to regulate it in school—
> beyond defining too much or too little of it as misbehavior
> and relegating most of it to the arts, PE, recess, and the
> extracurricular program.[3] . . . By separating emotion from
> logic and reason in the classroom, we've simplified school
> management and evaluation, but we've also then separated
> two sides of one coin—and lost something important in
> the process. It's impossible to separate emotion from the
> other important activities of life. Don't try.[4]

Sylwester goes on to outline six areas in which emotional and social learning must come together for the benefit of youth and schools:

- Accepting and controlling our emotions
- Using metacognitive activities
- Using activities that promote social interaction
- Using activities that provide an emotional context
- Avoiding intense emotional stress in school
- Recognizing the relationship between emotions and health

He also points out that the multiple intelligences are socially based and interrelated: "It's difficult to think of linguistic, musical, and interpersonal intelligence out of the context of social and cooperative activity, and the other four forms of intelligence—logical-mathematical, spatial, bodily-kinesthetic, even intrapersonal—are likewise principally social in normal practice."[5] Emotional competence is a critical, if not *the* critical, basis for intellectual pursuits. Considering the widespread perception that today's youth are more troubled emotionally, is it any wonder that schools are experiencing increasing difficulty in the pursuit of intellectual development?

Ways to manage behavior successfully rank at or near the top of everyone's wish list for schools. The search for new behavior management strategies should begin with a careful diagnosis of the causes of the problems. While it is easy to focus exclusively on students in addressing misbehavior, it must be recognized that student disruption and aggression do not occur in isolation. School discipline policies and practices, and teacher expectations and attitudes, can contribute to student misbehavior.[6] Research has shown that punitive discipline policies and practices such as suspensions, expulsions, and corporal punishment may exacerbate student discipline problems and lead to students' dropping out of school.[7] Negative teacher expectations and attitudes have a profound impact on students' school success.[8] Current school responses, which are largely punitive and reactive, are blocking the school's capacity to achieve its ultimate purpose—to advance each student's social, emotional, and academic development toward the goal of becoming an effective, responsible citizen. Attempts to control and punish children are improving neither children's behavior nor their emotional literacy. While punitive responses appeal to the general public, concerned that actions be taken to curb disruptive student behavior, punitive approaches often are ineffective or even counterproductive in curtailing that behavior.[9]

Herb Kohl, author and educator, talking in an interview about his latest book, *The Discipline of Hope*, says that "unless you project hope for your students, your efforts to teach them to read, write, and calculate won't make a profound difference. A teacher's task is not only to engage students' imagination but also to convince them that they are people of worth who can do something in a very difficult world. When children don't have access to resources, it is very easy for them to give up on hope. And if you give up on hope, what's the point of learning to read, etc.?"[10] In response to the query, How do you instill this capacity to hope? Kohl replies, "The first big thing that makes a difference is respect. If you don't respect the people you teach and you don't have a feeling that your students are of equal value to yourself—that they can become potentially almost anything—then you won't teach much to your students. Second, realize that humiliation is absolutely a sin when it comes to good teaching. You may have to figure out a new way to deal with kids who defy you, but humiliation has to go out the window."

An effective behavior management plan establishes clear expectations, develops a responsibility education program to teach those expectations, employs facilitative strategies to help individuals self-evaluate behavior, and provides a menu of acceptable behaviors from which an individual might choose. If the management plan is required to include prescribed behavioral consequences, logical ones are employed. The use of logical consequences is a powerful way for a manager to respond to misbehavior, not only effective in altering the behavior but respectful of the person exhibiting the behavior and useful in helping that person take responsibility for his or her actions. The belief underlying the use of logical consequences is that the individual, upon reflection and when helped to understand the expectations, will want to participate and do better. The view is that each learner is basically good but is often struggling to understand himself or herself, plus struggling to establish meaningful relationships with the adults in the school and with other learners. Each learner also has a life of pressures and uncertainties beyond school that may be occupying consciousness at any time in school. All students from time to time lose their control and make mistakes; using logical consequences rather than punishment and humiliation helps the student to fix mistakes and know what to do next time. The essence of the educational environment as a learning laboratory for the development of responsible behavior is exactly this. It is not the manager's job to make a learner feel bad about his or her behavior. Chances are that if the learner knows what is expected and knows he or she has misbehaved, the learner already feels bad. The manager's job is to help the learner choose a better course of action the next time. This book is about how to do that and why.

Whatever all the elements, the ultimate mission of our schools is to prepare our young people to participate fully and responsibly in our democratic society. These young people must be able to do that on their own through the exercise of responsible behavioral choices. Our society is not constructed, nor do we wish it to be constructed, with some authority always directing an individual's actions. The ability to deal constructively with the ever-present conflicts of life is central to one's future success as a citizen of this social order. Without the ability to resolve conflicts constructively, one will be constantly at the mercy of others. Without emotional intelligence, one cannot engage successfully in conflict resolution. To turn students into informed and involved members of our democratic society, educators need to create schools and classrooms with cooperation, participation, and support as the cornerstones.[11]

Education is living, not just the preparation for living. Students must be involved in dealing with real problems in order to learn what they need to know now and later. The fact is, students are involved with real problems constantly. When the school does not accept this fact and commit to teach students tools to deal with those problems, students and the school often disjoin. If students are provided opportunities to learn tools for personal problem solving and then are encouraged to solve their own real problems in the school environment, they will likely become more accepting of the school's efforts to expand their repertoire of information and skills in other areas of intellectual pursuit. Students will see school as creditable, relevant. They will see learning as pertinent to their lives—present and future. Conflict resolution can help to prevent the disassociation of students and school. Students can learn to resolve what they perceive to be real-life problems in constructive, need-fulfilling ways, yielding responsible learners in our schools and giving those learners a meaningful context to develop the attitudes, skills, and behaviors to be effective citizens in our communities, our nation, and our world. If young people do not learn to resolve problems constructively while in our schools, where will this learning occur?

It is possible to learn to live in civil association with one another. Doing so means not only learning how to work and live with others, but also learning how to disagree—respectfully. Learning to live constructively with conflict requires the opportunity to practice behaviors in a significant life context—school can be, probably must be, that context for youth today. When that occurs, emotionally intelligent schools and classrooms will be a reality. Emotionally intelligent schools and classrooms bring to life the vision of the peaceable school:

> Imagine a school or classroom where the learners manage and resolve their own conflicts, both with and without adult assistance. Picture a place where diversity and individuality are celebrated . . . a place where people listen in order to understand others' viewpoints and perceive conflict as an opportunity to learn and grow . . . a place where feelings are openly expressed, even anger and frustration, in ways that are not aggressive or destructive . . . a place where adults and children cooperate instead of acting aggressively or coercively . . . a place that supports everyone's rights and encourages everyone to exercise his or her responsibilities . . . a place where peace is viewed as an active process, made day by day, moment by moment.[12]

This book is about one dimension of schools and classrooms that is critical to realizing this vision: behavior management. Addressing this dimension alone will not bring to life this vision for most schools. This book does not address, in depth, another critical dimension. Schools must concern themselves with curricular issues, what is to be delivered to youth and how it is to be delivered, to ensure that youth are engaged in quality learning, as outlined in *The School for Quality Learning: Managing the School and Classroom the Deming Way*.[13] An effective behavior management program must explore whether adult requests, whether stemming from personal desire or the system's expectation, are reasonable and age appropriate. More generally, the review must take into account how the environment created by adults might contribute to student response. What must not be conspicuous by its absence from such a review is the school curriculum. Kohn asserts that "a huge proportion of unwelcome behaviors can be traced to a problem with what students are being asked to learn."[14] How do we create a meaningful curriculum that stretches learners' thinking, elicits their curiosity, and helps them reflect more skillfully on questions that are already important to them? A full response to this query is beyond the scope of this book. The point is, there is a connection between the learning program defined by the curriculum and student behavior. As Kohn queries, "When students are 'off task', our first response should be to ask, 'What's the task?'"[15]

The omission of curricular issues from this current book is in no way intended to suggest that all is relatively well on this front in our schools. Educators must address three fundamental questions:

- Is what we are asking young people to do in our schools actually learning?

- Is what we are asking youth to learn in our schools actually worth learning?

- If it is worth learning, have we made it clear to youth why what we are teaching is worth learning?

All too often the response of young people to each of these three questions is a resounding "no." "No, this stuff is just busy work." "No, I'll never use this stuff; nobody I know uses it." "No, this is what you do in school—it has nothing to do with my life except for school." These responses help us understand the unwillingness of an increasing percentage of youth to participate in our schools as we would like. They see little if any connection between what school offers and their own basic needs. Students' unwillingness to participate then often becomes the entry point for our disciplinary procedures. Changing behavior management practices alone will do little to ameliorate an underlying lack of perceived meaning in the curriculum. Glasser claims that "to focus on discipline is to ignore the real problem. We will never be able to get students (or anyone else) to be in good order if, day after day, we try to force them to do what they do not find satisfying"[16]

Clearly, schools should provide training and practice in conflict resolution. Conflict resolution education is addressed in this book because constructive conflict resolution is a hallmark of the emotionally intelligent, and because most, if not all, of what is classified as misbehavior in schools is actually conflict for which constructive resolutions have not yet been advanced. Conflict resolution enables youth to learn to resolve disputes constructively and peaceably and thus is a prime vehicle for practicing emotional intelligence. A training program to educate youth in conflict resolution is presented in *Creating the Peaceable School: A Comprehensive Program for Teaching Conflict Resolution.*[17]

Endnotes

1. H. Weisinger, *Emotional Intelligence at Work* (San Francisco: Jossey-Bass, 1998).

2. D. Goleman, *Emotional Intelligence* (New York: Bantam, 1995).

3. R. Sylwester, *A Celebration of Neurosis: An Educator's Guide to the Human Brain* (Alexandria, VA: Association for Supervision and Curriculum Development, 1995), 95.

4. Sylwester, *A Celebration of Neurosis*, 75

5. Sylwester, *A Celebration of Neurosis*, 77.

6. D. R. Dupper and C. H. Krishef, "School-Based Social-Cognitive Skills Training for Middle School Students with School Behavior Problems," *Children and Youth Services Review 15* (1993), 131–142.

7. L. M. DeRidder, "How Suspension and Expulsion Contribute to Dropping Out," *The Education Digest 56* (1990), 44–47; G. B. Bauer, R. Dubanoski, L. A.Yamauchi, and K. A. M. Honbo, "Corporal Punishment and the Schools," *Education and Urban Society 22* (1990), 285–290.

8. V. Paredes and L. Frazer, *School Climate in AISD* (Austin, TX: Austin Independent School District, ERIC Document Reproduction Service No. ED 353 677, 1992); P. Gandara, " 'Those' Children Are Ours: Moving toward Community," *Equity and Choice 12* (1989), 5–12; D. S. Pollard, "The Resurgence of Racism: Reducing the Impact of Racism on Students," *Educational Leadership 47* (1989), 73–75.

9. L. Brendtro and N. Long, "Breaking the Cycle of Conflict," *Educational Leadership 52* (1995), 52–55.

10. M. Scherer, "A Conversation with Herb Kohl," *Educational Leadership 56* (1998), 9.

11. R. J. Bodine and D. K. Crawford, "Democratizing Schools: Bridging School Behavioral Expectations and Responsible Citizenship in All Life Contexts," *The Fourth R 83* (1998), 5.

12. R. J. Bodine, D. K. Crawford, and F. Schrumpf, *Creating the Peaceable School: A Comprehensive Program for Teaching Conflict Resolution* (Champaign, IL: Research Press, 1994), 1.

13. D. K. Crawford, R. J. Bodine, and R. G. Hoglund, *The School for Quality Learning: Managing the School and Classroom the Deming Way* (Champaign, IL: Research Press, 1993).

14. A. Kohn, *Beyond Discipline: From Compliance to Community* (Alexandria, VA: Association for Supervision and Curriculum Development, 1996), 18.

15. Kohn, *Beyond Discipline,* 19.

16. W. Glasser, *Control Theory in the Classroom* (New York: Harper and Row, 1986), 12.

17. Bodine et al., *Creating the Peaceable School.*

CHAPTER 1

Our Collective Emotional Crisis

It was a radiant Midwestern fall morning, the kind of crisp day that energizes just about everyone. We were observing third and fourth graders in their multiage classroom and were astonished by their lack of zest and harmony. When arranging to visit this urban elementary school, we asked the principal to arrange for us to visit classrooms that were exemplary, especially ones with good emotional climates and positive teacher-student relationships. Through such classroom observations, we hoped to discern some specific examples of practices supporting the development of emotional intelligence in the classroom. The principal urged us to visit this particular classroom, citing it as "one of the best" learner-centered classrooms in the state. She noted that the experienced teacher was a staff development provider within the school district, training other educators in classroom management strategies and in the use of individualized learning programs. She was also on the state's master teacher roster. In short, our observations were conducted in a "better than average" classroom managed by a master teacher. During our morning observation, we witnessed the following scenarios:

- Alex and Sandra engage in property destruction by deliberately breaking colored pencils belonging to Nate. Nate complains to the teacher, who is working with a small group at the science center.

- Two minutes after the teacher calls the students to a whole-class meeting, only 8 of 26 students are in place attending to the teacher as she introduces the activity.

- Brandon and Reggie bully Robert into letting them use his video football game.

- Shania and Rose refuse to share the math materials in the math center with Rachel. Rachel had asked, "Can I have some of the attribute blocks?" Rose replied, "No, we were here first." The math center's posted rules stated that four students are allowed in that center at any one time.

- During a 15-minute independent work period, eight different students are observed checking with the teacher to see if they are doing "the right thing"; two of those students do so three times each.

- Donald and Marcy refuse to do what the teacher assistant asks them to do when she directs them to a specific activity. Marcy says, "You're not my teacher!"

- Nikki leaves the reading corner in tears, then complains to the teacher that Evie has been teasing her.

- During an interactive work period, when students are working at learning centers in the classroom, usually in small groups, six different verbal exchanges that were put-downs or name-calling occur.

- Michael tries to get another student to work with him on an assignment and is rejected by four different individuals; he goes to a corner of the room and just sits.

- During the whole-class meeting, several students aggressively compete for the teacher's attention, interrupting others and physically crowding others to get closer to the teacher.

- Also during this class meeting, two students in the back of the group exchange racial slurs, then shove each other; the teacher tells them to separate.

- During an instructional small group, students generally do not listen when another student presents an idea. When the teacher asks the group what Mario said, no one responds. The teacher asks Mario to repeat his idea.

- Five minutes into an independent work period, only six students are engaged in one of several tasks that the teacher has suggested as appropriate for that work period.

- No student is observed reading independently during the work period; it is one of the teacher-suggested options.

- Three students argue over the use of a computer; the posted class rule is only two students at that station at any time.

- Donald is observed sleeping during a whole-class instructional activity.

- No student responds to the teacher's questions during a small-group discussion of a literature book they were to have read; when the teacher reframes the question, students are still silent.

- Over half of the students have brought no current event example to share; this assignment had been given 3 days earlier.

- Quiet reading is not quiet; the teacher reminds the class on four occasions within 10 minutes that it is a quiet reading period.

Despite our overall positive general impression of this classroom, these examples of inappropriate or nonproductive behaviors were not isolated intrusions into the learning environment, nor were they exhibited by only three or four "problem" students. Imagine the proliferation of these observable incidents in other classrooms, especially those in which the teacher-student relationship is not as strong as it is here—we did note that this teacher and these students appeared to enjoy a mutually respectful relationship and that the teacher seemed very skilled at accepting each student while also challenging each to learn.

Perhaps it was the contrast to the beautiful day outside that brought such clarity to this microcosm. Educators have a critical window of opportunity for influencing the essential emotional habits of children that govern their future lives, and, for the large part, this potential is ineffectively refined in most classrooms.

As we observed this classroom, the teacher and her assistant seemed constantly to be managing the behaviors of the students. An essential and observable feature of every classroom and every school is the behavior management program. Behavior management is the necessary and critical responsibility of those in charge at the classroom or schoolwide level, in order to create the learning environment. Since behavior is closely linked to emotion, the format and operation of the behavior management program is directly linked to social and emotional development. The challenge is, Can behavior management strategies be designed and employed to *facilitate* the students' development of emotional competence and responsibility?

Responsible versus Compliant Behavior

When one accepts that being responsible is not the same as being compliant, the necessity for a shift in behavior management strategies becomes inarguable. Toward this acceptance, consider that a compliant individual chooses to behave in a certain manner because of external forces, conditions, or influences; a responsible individual chooses to behave according to reasonable and acceptable standards because of internal need satisfaction and concern for self and others. Which individual is more likely to exhibit appropriate, productive behavior when not directly supervised by a person in authority? A responsible individual assertively challenges standards that are perceived as unreasonable or unacceptable; a compliant individual with similar perceptions that a request or requirement is unreasonable or unacceptable is likely to avoid such challenges or react aggressively—passively or actively—especially toward those thought to be in control. Which individual is more likely to effect a positive change in the human condition for self and for others?

Assertiveness is a basic life skill. Assertiveness is knowing how to take advantage of opportunities without victimizing another, knowing how to resist pressure or intimidation from others without destroying relationships or isolating oneself, and knowing how to resolve conflicts in ways that make use of the full range of non-violent opportunities that exist. Assertiveness and aggressiveness are very different. Assertiveness skills not only combat violence, they are also necessary for a quality life. An assertive individual is emotionally intelligent; an aggressive individual likely is not. Responsibility and assertiveness are complementary. Acquiescence is not responsibility, yet compliance frequently demands acquiescence. Compliance may be forced or coerced; responsibility can be developed only through appropriate education and free choice. Is the mission of schools to develop responsible individuals or compliant ones?

Learning Transfer

Effective educational practices are based upon the knowledge that human beings learn, remember, and think. They also plan, solve problems, and use language. They can, and usually do, learn to modify their behavior when confronted with new situations. Human beings are capable of generalizing prior learning to differing circumstances. They pursue the acquisition of concepts and strategies to cope with both current and anticipated events. This flexible, adaptive character of human behavior illustrates the significance of learning and provides the basic rationale for learning to be emotionally intelligent. Through learning, we acquire our capacity to behave in a variety of circumstances, always driven by the goal of attaining satisfaction from the experience. Quite simply, emotional intelligence is the intelligent use of emotions. Emotional intelligence is a necessary antecedent to successful conflict resolution, and constructive conflict resolution is an indicator of an emotionally intelligent being. Since conflict is perpetually present, every circumstance affords the opportunity to manage conflict, and each individual is required to do so. In short, every individual will learn to do something with conflict. Unfortunately, many have no personal experiences from which to draw or no models from which to learn other than the mostly dysfunctional approaches to conflict of "flight" or "fight." Their only way of gaining satisfaction from experiences involving conflict is to try harder at what they do know—flee faster or farther, or fight longer and harder. Meeting basic needs often involves choosing behaviors that result in the victimization of others.

Developing emotional intelligence and learning the problem-solving strategies of conflict resolution provide behavioral alternatives to "flight" or "fight" that may be chosen to effectively manage conflicts or disputes. These alternatives are self-enhancing and socially responsible. At first, the attainment of this purpose may appear to be simply a matter of providing skills training in problem-solving processes sufficient so that what is learned is remembered. However, achieving the goal of choosing different behaviors in conflict situations entails much more than basic skills training. Each new situation the individual confronts contains unique elements and requires that individual to use previous learning in a new way. Thus, the individual must not only be able to remember, but must also be able to select from his or her experiences those responses that are most appropriate. When what has been learned is creatively employed in new situations, transfer of learning has been achieved. Transfer is highly unlikely unless the individual has a deep and profound understanding of why the problem-solving process is constructed the way it is. In other words, transfer is likely when one is emotionally intelligent and when one is equipped with tools to behave responsibly. One who follows a procedure simply as a ritual, established through repeated practice, is unlikely to apply the procedure to circumstances that he or she perceives as different. Whereas it is possible to train individuals to follow a technique, it requires education for the individual to learn when to apply the technique and how to modify the technique to fit varying circumstances. Education can yield emotionally intelligent beings who through the processes of self-evaluation exhibit the competencies of self-awareness, self-control, and empathy, and who act in socially responsible ways by exhibiting the arts of listening, resolving conflicts, and cooperating. An emotionally intelligent individual will achieve personal need satisfaction without denying need satisfaction to others.

It is impossible to predict exactly in what situations a person will use the problem-solving strategies of conflict resolution. Nevertheless, it is clear that these strategies are "life skills," and the view that conflict resolution provides skills for living stipulates transfer of learning. Understanding conflict and peacemaking allows one to assimilate the perceptions of an unknown circumstance into the framework of known responses and to integrate the two, generating unique but socially acceptable behaviors. This ability to assimilate, integrate, and generate is the hallmark of an emotionally intelligent being. Emotional intelligence encompasses many of the foundation abilities that an individual must possess before that individual is able to successfully employ conflict resolution processes. Developing emotional intelligence to enable a young person to learn conflict resolution is simply adding other tools to use, especially when involved in interpersonal conflicts. Having only the paintbrush to gloss over conflict, to pretend that it is something it isn't or that it can be hidden, or the sledge hammer to beat it into submission offers one little hope for personal need satisfaction or for productive associations. Could education be viewed as a process of more fully equipping each individual's toolbox?

The development of social and emotional competencies does not occur in isolation. Developing these competencies requires an investment of time and energy. Integrating the development of emotional intelligence and the behavior management program sets the behaviors to be learned into a framework of relevance and provides for efficiency—the time invested in managing behavior is more likely also to be time invested in learning. The social and emotional competencies become behaviors to practice in order to live in civil association with others in the environment. Developing these competencies involves appropriate learning activities for all youth, not just those who exhibit disruptive behavior. The view that if one is not disruptive one has emotional intelligence may be comforting to those who wish to continue the status quo, but the view is not valid. The same is true of the view that all who are disruptive lack emotional intelligence. Compliant individuals are rarely disruptive, at least in the presence of a management authority; responsible individuals may be seen as disruptive, especially by a management authority, within a system that is unresponsive to their individual needs.

Today's Behavioral Scene

Unfortunately, the development of emotional intelligence is not a priority in most schools, and educators are experiencing the ramifications. Feelings of frustration and hopelessness have become deeply ingrained among educators, who increasingly find themselves overwhelmed by students who are disruptive, disrespectful, irresponsible, and violent. In recent years across the country, school districts—urban, suburban, and rural—have reported increases in suspensions for weapons violations, assault and battery of staff and of other students, and other offenses and rule violations. The number of calls to police departments for school-related incidents as well as dropout and force-out rates are also on the incline. These trends are indicative of pervasive problems that touch every school and neighborhood, cutting across race, religion, and gender.

Evidence of this pervasiveness, the Tennessee Department of Education's Youth Risk Behavior Survey of 1995 and 1997 indicates that 14% of the students in 1995 and 12% in 1997 said they did not go to school on one or more of the 30 days preceding the survey because they felt threatened or had actually been threatened or injured with a weapon on school property during the previous 12 months.[1] In addition, 13% of the 1995 and 14% of the 1997 respondents said they had traded blows during the past 12 months. Statistical data on suspensions and expulsions for violent offenses gathered by Tennessee educational officials in 1997 also showed the following:

- For violence or threatened violence, suspensions were up 10.53%, expulsions up 45.66%.

- Fighting among students, suspensions up 6.7%, expulsions up 41.72%.

- Possession/use of weapons (excluding firearms), suspensions up 13.02%, expulsions up 41.75%.

- Possession/use of a firearm, suspensions down 36.82%, expulsions down 31%.

Although some of the Tennessee data trends reflect the impact of zero tolerance policies implemented between 1995 and 1997, it is evident that violent offenses are increasing. Tennessee is certainly not unique, nor likely even a national leader in these statistical categories. It is noteworthy that the state of Tennessee recently launched a proactive statewide initiative to create peaceable schools through a collaborative partnership between the William J. Harbison Law-Related Education Foundation and the Tennessee Department of Education.

Perhaps these last few school years have provided a national wake-up call on youth violence. High-profile media reports from various sources have borne witness to incidents in which youth-perpetrated gun violence on school campuses or at school events claimed student and adult lives:

- February 2, 1996: At Frontier Junior High School in Moses Lake, Washington, the teacher and two students are killed and a third student wounded when a 14-year-old enters an algebra class and opens fire with a hunting rifle he concealed in a trench coat.

- February 19, 1997: The principal and a student are killed and two students wounded when a 16-year-old opens fire with a shotgun in a common area at the Bethel, Alaska, high school.

- October 1, 1997: A 16-year-old in Pearl, Mississippi, is accused of killing his mother, then going to Pearl High School and shooting nine students. Two die, including the suspect's ex-girlfriend.

- December 1, 1997: Three students are killed and five others wounded in a prayer circle in a hallway before classes were scheduled to begin at Heath High School in West Paducah, Kentucky. A 14-year-old student of the school is arrested.

- March 24, 1998: Four girls and a teacher are shot to death and ten others wounded during a false fire alarm at Westside Middle School in Jonesboro, Arkansas. Two boys, ages 11 and 13, are accused of setting the alarm and then opening fire from a nearby woods.

- April 24, 1998: A science teacher is shot to death in front of students at a graduation dance in Edinboro, Pennsylvania. A 14-year-old student of James W. Parker Middle School is charged.

- May 19, 1998: Three days before his graduation, an 18-year-old honor student opens fire in a parking lot at Lincoln County High School in Fayetteville, Tennessee, killing a classmate who allegedly was dating his ex-girlfriend.

- May 21, 1998: A 17-year-old student is killed and more than 20 other people wounded after a 15-year-old boy opens fire at Thurston High School in Springfield,

Oregon. Following his apprehension at the school, the bodies of his parents are found at home.

- June 15, 1998: A teacher/coach and an adult volunteer aide are both wounded in Richmond, Virginia, when a 14-year-old opens fire in a crowded hallway outside Armstrong High School's main office during final exams week. Neither adult is wounded fatally; allegedly, neither was the shooter's intended target.

- April 20, 1999: Two students, ages 17 and 18, in a prolonged siege of Columbine High School in Littleton, Colorado, kill a teacher and 12 students before killing themselves. Several others inside the school were wounded during the shooting and bombing rampage.

- May 20, 1999: A 15-year-old student opens fire in a commons area just before classes were scheduled to begin at Heritage High School in Conyers, Georgia. Six students were injured in this shooting spree.

These shocking events captured attention because they occurred in the sanctity of schools. Although violence has visited the schoolgrounds before, it either occurred in urban schools or was perpetrated by an outsider to the school. These incidents are unique because of their sheer number, the identities of the perpetrators, and their locations. The perpetrators were all white and were students of the school. The school locations were rural, suburban, or small town. These cases reveal that youth violence transcends economic status and ethnicity. No longer are the inner cities and urban settings of the United States alone vulnerable to this type of random violence.

Furthermore, these were only a few of the incidents of gun violence by youth. As reported in the annual PRIDE survey, 973,000 students in grades 6 through 12 carried a gun to school during the 1997–1998 school year, and 45% of those students went to school armed on six or more occasions.[2] PRIDE, the Parent Resource Institute for Drug Education, a nonprofit drug prevention program, has conducted the survey annually for the past 11 years. Other findings from the survey were as follows:

- Sixty-four percent of those 973,000 who reported carrying a gun admitted using an illegal drug on a monthly basis.

- Fifty-one percent of the 973,000 said they had threatened to harm a teacher; 63% had threatened to harm a student.

- Of the 973,000, 59% were white, 18% black, 12% Hispanic, 3% Asian, and 3% Native American.

- Students who did not carry guns were 53% more likely to be involved in after-school programs and 34% more likely to participate in school activities.

Startlingly, the potential for disaster is immense even if these statistics are considered inflated. What happened in Jonesboro, Littleton, and other locations could have happened anywhere.

Although obviously not the only victims, young people especially are victimized in staggering numbers by youth violence—many youth die annually at the hands of other youth. In addition, staggering numbers of youth are victimized nonfatally by youth physical violence. Larger numbers still are victimized by psychological violence between and among youth. Youth involvement in and with violence is a universal problem. In this population, physical aggression and intimidation are often the first response to problems and disagreements. The potential for and actuality of youth violence are too large for increased security measures and increased supervision alone to deter or control. As pervasive as these behaviors appear to be, the goal of eliminating physical violence seems insufficient. Could the goal not be to work together for a common good, to learn not only how to agree, but also how to disagree constructively?

There are no simple solutions, and there are no small target populations. In the days before the fatal shooting at Westside Middle School in Jonesboro, Arkansas, say children who survived, the two boys charged in the killings made clear in verbal threats and by wielding weapons that they planned a massacre at the school to avenge a slight against them. But rather than speak up, said witnesses, they either didn't believe the threats or felt uncomfortable reporting them to an adult. The scenario in

Edinboro, Pennsylvania, a month later was similar. The threats of the 14-year-old charged in a prom killing were considered by peers to be without credibility, thus unworthy of reporting. In the Alaska incident, authorities formally accused two other students of knowing the shootings would take place. In all of the cases described here, a common thread is that, after the fact, others reported either knowing or suspecting that the action was planned. Another common thread revealed by the investigations is that each of the perpetrators lacked the coping skills necessary to deal with the natural letdowns of adolescent life.

Overcoming failures to communicate real and perceived threats and understanding the depth of youth passions are keys to reduc-ing the violence in schools—both physical violence and psychological trespass. Making students equal partners in identifying the roots of conflict and providing them with the tools to deal constructively with those conflicts seems the only viable course of action. Imperative also is the creation of a climate in which young people see the adults in charge as a source of help. Young people will be more likely to report troubled peers, or peers with troubling thoughts, to an adult if they have assurance that these individuals will receive help instead of being expunged or punished. As adults, we are often out of touch with what is important to our youth. Kids worry about things that would not even occur to us as being problems, let alone problems worthy of violence. The teasing in the shower, the insults, the pressure to be a particular way—these are the things students must live with every day as well as things that often set them off.

In his study of violence among middle and high school students, Daniel Lockwood reports three key findings:[3]

- In the largest portion of violent incidents—an act carried out with the intention, or perceived intention, of physically injuring another person—the "opening move" involved a relatively minor affront but escalated from there. Few of these initiating actions by student, student antagonist, or third party were predatory.

- The largest number of incidents took place among young people who knew one another, and the school or the home was the place where most incidents began.

- The most common goal of the violent action was retribution, and the justifications and excuses offered indicated the impulse stemmed not from an absence of values but from a well-developed value system in which violence is acceptable.

Lockwood concludes that reducing the occurrence of opening moves appears to be the most promising approach to preventing escalation to violence. The study found the most common of these affronts to be as follows:

- Unprovoked offensive touching—bumps, hits, slaps, pushes, grabs, shoves, and so on (13%)
- Interfering with a possession owned or being used (13%)
- Request to do something (10%)
- Backbiting—something bad is said and gets back to the person discussed (9%)
- Play—playful verbal teasing and put-downs or rough physical play (9%)
- Insults—not meant to be playful (7%)

Would an emotionally intelligent individual likely escalate these incidents?

If young people see adults accepting violence as a good solution to a problem, then they will emulate that violence. Lockwood's finding on the excuses offered supports this contention. Adult influence can come from the home, the media, the church, the school, and any other place where youth have the opportunity to observe adults in action. What do youth see of the adults? Where are the visible models of successful problem solving and conflict resolution? Modeling has two dimensions: First, the behavior must occur, and second, it must be observable to others. Obviously, adults who use constructive conflict resolution exist. Do young people see that happening? What is the frequency of those observations versus the frequency of observations of dysfunctional behavior in conflict situations? There does appear to be one absolute: We cannot prevent violence with violence. Does it make any sense to talk about zero tolerance of violence in a violent society? It seems logical to offer young people who are the potential perpetrators of violence a more attractive way of using their intelligence, energy, and efforts, as well as of venting their frustration and rage.

Much is made of statistics on rising student suspensions, expulsions, and legally reportable offenses occurring within schools as evidence of changing student behavior, and the increasing difficulty in providing education in our schools is viewed as a result of that behavior change. Educators decry the unmanageable nature of children, even the very youngest in our schools. Little is detailed about tailoring responses to the ways in which students are different. Rarely is attention paid, at least among policy makers, to *why* current youth programs are not working or even *how* current programs might be contributing to the problems. There exists instead a loud and persistent clamoring to develop more stringent punitive measures to manage the environment and more alternatives to remove those who do not respond from the classroom, the school, even the community. Discipline has been one of the highest priorities of schools for several years, and today discipline problems continue largely unabated and unresolved. Why do these problems persist? Can they be resolved? We believe they can. One thing is certain, however—punishing youth for not having learned that which has not been taught will not contribute to resolution and likely will exacerbate existing problems.

Analyses of disciplinary problems in schools reveal several recurring messages. One is that the frequency and severity of infractions correlate positively with the ethnicity and gender of students, with African American males currently being affected most significantly and with Hispanic males not far behind. In nearly every multiethnic school system, these groups have a disproportionately high percentage of serious disciplinary actions—suspensions and expulsions. Second, as grade level increases, so does the frequency of disciplinary problems for the students affected. This factor, coupled with the reported increase in suspensions even of kindergarten-age students, would indicate that the trend for schools is increasing numbers of discipline problems. Third, students with major disciplinary problems do not perform well academically, perhaps partly because they are frequently separated from instructional interactions. Fourth, past and present efforts to resolve discipline problems have been largely ineffective, and some of those efforts have actually intensified the difficulties. Fifth, many students remain unidentified as discipline problems simply because their inappropriate and nonproductive behaviors do not significantly impact others—either the teacher or other students.

Youth are crying out to us to do something. When their anguish was silent or self-directed, we did not respond with sustained vigor and concern. But now their feelings are turning outward. They are enraged, disenfranchised, and they feel they have little to lose, perhaps no future to compromise. The solution is there for us to see: Schools must be places where all children feel valued, useful, and needed.[4] If youth are not in a supportive environment outside of school, and many are not, then schools must develop effective ways to compensate while other systems work toward changing problematic conditions. What we cannot do is throw away any more generations of children by waiting and hoping for things to get better or for other systems to rescue us. Schools must stop pretending that someone is sending them the wrong students and if better students would just start to show up, then schools could once again function as they were intended. We have the students we have; there are no others to replace them. Schools exist to provide education in the present that will equip students to live productive lives in the new millenium. Achieving that goal likely has a great deal more to do with equipping students to be emotionally intelligent and lifelong learners than with imparting knowledge. What proactive measures can we take to improve our current state of affairs and also to prepare students for the mostly unknown future? Can schools be a place to learn appropriate behaviors through exploration and practice, rather than simply a place to behave appropriately?

Focusing concern and action on occurrences of physical violence, the national modus operandi adopted by most schools, is treating a symptom and offers little for the future. Focusing concern and action on educating students toward alternatives to violence, in all their various forms, offers hope that, more and more frequently, those alternatives will be the behaviors of choice. Such education demands more than telling youth to "just say no." Such education provides opportunities to learn and practice self-awareness, self-control, empathy, cooperation, and constructive conflict resolution. Such education actually may succeed in developing a national consciousness without violence as a primary strategy for seeking individual need satisfaction. It is not enough to convince youth not to hit, shoot, or physically harass; youth need the ability to live in harmony with others—even with those who are different. Is it not likely that even those students now succeeding in our schools could profit directly, as well as indirectly, from such learning opportunities?

Since violence—pervasively psychological trespass and, increasingly, physical trespass—manifested among youth is the observable result of unresolved conflict, and since acts of violence are occurring with increasing frequency within schools, schools are naturally expected to provide prevention programs. The best school-based violence prevention programs seek to do more than reach the individual child. They instead try to change the total school environment, to create a safe community whose members live by a credo of nonviolence and multicultural appreciation.[5] One short-term goal of educational institutions must be to move students from simply recognizing that they live in a multicultural, often violent society to feeling prepared to contribute and live peacefully in their diverse communities. Looking ahead, educators and educational systems must challenge young people to believe and act on the understanding that a nonviolent, pluralistic society is a realistic goal. It is not just what youth are taught in the classroom that reinforces the messages of nonviolence and respect for diversity, but also what they experience as the commitments and values of the institutions and adults in their lives.[6] It is an insufficient goal for young people to stop hitting and shooting or otherwise physically abusing one another; the goal must be to help young people care about themselves and about others. Only then will living in civil association with others characterize future generations.

The Role of Schools

Schools alone likely cannot change a violent society. However, for today's youth, school is the last collective experience. In what else do all youths participate in our society? Schools thus have a unique opportunity to forge a vision of a nonviolent future and likely are the only institution in which youth can learn and develop the behaviors necessary to realize that vision. In fact, is it not the mission of the United States' school system to prepare youth to participate effectively in our democratic society? To realize this vision, schools must do as follows:

- Stop making the problems worse—stop failing students, stop suspending and expelling students, thus denying them the opportunities they most need, and stop otherwise alienating youth from the learning environment.

- Teach alternatives to violence—real strategies to satisfy individual needs without victimizing others.

- Teach students to act responsibly in social settings—use the school setting as a laboratory to study both appropriate and inappropriate behavior and to increase the number of behavioral options for each student.

- Teach students to understand and accept the consequences of their behavior.

- Improve the quality of learning.

Where, if not in our schools, will the critical mass of our country's youth develop emotional intelligence?

The goal of making the school a safe haven in which youth can gain respite from violence in order to think and learn is a good one. But it cannot be created apart from improving what and how teachers teach, changing how school rules are administered, and working toward a nonviolent vision shared by everyone in the building. Making schools safe havens is not likely to stamp out violence in society, but that should not deter us from the effort.[7] Making schools safe havens, from both physical and psychological trespass, may have a much more pervasive influence on the future than we dare hope.

Schools need to pay attention, not reactively, but proactively, to the development of social and emotional competencies. These competencies are the ability to understand, manage, and express the social and emotional aspects of one's life in ways that enable the successful management of life tasks such as learning, forming relationships, solving everyday problems, and adapting to the complex demands of growth, development, and change. They include self-awareness, control of impulsivity, working cooperatively, and caring about oneself and about others. The importance of these competencies for successful academic learning is supported by emerging insights from the field of neuropsychology. Many elements of learning are relational, or based on relationships, and social and emotional skills are essential for the successful development of thinking and learning activities that have traditionally been considered cognitive. Processes that have been considered pure thinking are now seen as phenomena in which the cognitive and emotional aspects work synergistically. Brain studies show that memory is coded to specific events and linked to social and emotional situations, and the latter are integral parts of larger units of memory that make up what is learned and retained, including what takes place in the classroom.[8]

In order for children to become responsible, compassionate citizens in a pluralistic, democratic society, they must not only be taught the skills necessary to handle differences effectively and nonviolently, but also be given the opportunity to utilize these skills daily in the classroom, in the school, and in the community. In an emotionally intelligent classroom, children and adults manage and resolve conflicts by negotiating, mediating, and participating in group problem solving. These strategies, learned by everyone in the school community, should be a part of a comprehensive student and staff development program. Central to such a program is the implementation of a noncoercive discipline system designed to encourage student self-discipline and responsibility. In the final analysis, behavior is changed only when one's own assessment and evaluation determines the need for change. In a noncoercive system, the behavioral self-assessment standard becomes, What type of person do I want to be? or What kind of community do I want to help create? rather than, What do they want me to do, and what happens to me if I don't do it (the behavioral assessment standard in punitive systems)? or What do they want me to do, and what do I get if I do it (the behavioral assessment standard for external rewards)?

Emotional Crisis

Young people themselves seem to recognize that they are at risk. Many factors influence why some young people have successes in life and why others have a harder time. Economic circumstances, genetics, trauma, and many other factors which the individual has little power to change play a role. Research by Search Institute, based in Minneapolis, has identified 40 developmental assets—concrete, positive experiences and qualities—that have tremendous influence on young people's lives.[9] These are things that can be nurtured. The research shows that the 40 developmental assets help young people make wise decisions, choose positive paths, and grow up competent, caring, and responsible. These assets are grouped into eight categories:

1. Support: Young people need to experience support, care, and love from their families and from others. They need organizations and institutions that provide positive, supportive environments. (6 assets)

2. Empowerment: Young people need to be valued by their community and have opportunities to contribute to others. For this to occur, they must be safe and feel secure. (4 assets)

3. Boundaries and expectations: Young people need to know what is expected of them and whether activities and behaviors are "in bounds" or "out of bounds." (6 assets)

4. Constructive use of time: Young people need constructive, enriching opportunities for growth through creative activities, youth programs, quality time at home, and constructive involvement with other youth and adults. (4 assets)

5. Commitment to learning: Young people need to develop a life-long commitment to education and learning. (5 assets)

6. Positive values: Youth need to develop strong values that guide their choices. (6 assets)

7. Social competencies: Young people need skills and competencies that equip them to make positive choices, to build relationships, and to succeed in life. (5 assets)

8. Positive identity: Young people need a strong sense of their own power, purpose, worth, and promise. (4 assets)

Based on surveys conducted by the Search Institute of nearly 100,000 young people in grades 6 through 12 in 213 communities in 25 states during the 1996–1997 school year, young people report on average experiencing only 18 of 40 of these developmental assets.[10] While these assets are powerful influences on young people's lives and choices, 25 of the 40 assets were experienced by fewer than half of the young people surveyed. Ideally, to be emotionally enabled, all youth would experience at least 31 of these 40 assets. In this large sample, only 8% experienced 31 or more, while 62% experienced fewer than 20.

Yes, a collective emotional crisis exists with and for our future citizens. It is our adult responsibility to do something about it. It seems clear that schools must be major players in any action plan formulated to confront this crisis. Dr. David Hamburg, a psychiatrist and president of the Carnegie Corporation, an organization that has evaluated some pioneering emotional-educational programs, sees the years of transition into elementary school and again into middle school as marking two crucial points in a child's adjustment. For ages 6 to 11, says Hamburg, "School is a crucible and a defining experience that will heavily influence children's adolescence and beyond. A child's self-worth depends substantially on his or her ability to achieve in school. A child who fails in school sets in motion the self-defeating attitudes that can dim prospects for an entire lifespan."[11] Among the essentials for profiting from school, Hamburg notes, are the abilities to postpone gratification, to be socially responsible in appropriate ways, to maintain control over emotions, and to have an optimistic outlook—in other words, emotional intelligence. Would it not perhaps be more productive to implement a zero-tolerance for failure policy than a zero-tolerance for potential violent behavior policy?

If not the view of individual educators, the system of school as a whole is structured by a narrow view of intelligence, measured as IQ, a genetic given that cannot be changed by life experience and that largely fixes one's destiny in life. Daniel Goleman argues that the challenging question is "What can we change that will help our children fare better in life? What factors are at play, for example, when people of high IQ flounder and those of modest IQ do surprisingly well?"[12] Goleman also contends that the difference between success and failure quite often lies in self-control, zeal and persistence, and the ability to motivate oneself, the abilities he calls emotional intelligence. These skills can be taught to children, giving them a better chance to use whatever intellectual potential the genetic lottery has given them. The emotional lessons children learn at home and at school shape their emotional circuits, making them more adept—or inept—at the basics of emotional intelligence. Childhood and adolescence are critical windows of opportunity for developing the essential emotional habits that will govern one's life journey.

Clearly, schools impact the future by the learning opportunities they provide. As educators, we have a clear choice regarding those opportunities and thus our future. We can continue to limit the mission of school to intellectual development, likely destining the school to a continuing struggle for viability. Alternatively, we can recognize that continual emotional distress creates deficits in intellectual abilities, crippling students' capacity to learn. We can accept that our student population, for whatever reasons, is increasingly subject to emotional distress. Schools are receiving an increasingly higher percentage of children at risk for problems of academic failure, substance abuse, and criminality—not because of their intellectual deficiencies, but mostly because of impaired control over their emotional lives. If educators are unprepared or unwilling to address the collective emotional crisis in our schools, how will a future of civility ever be possible for the next generations? Educators can actively promote the development of emotional intelligence by, first, developing and implementing changes in their schools that promote emotionally healthy interactions among the constituency and, second, by providing all individuals learning opportunities that strengthen and reinforce the traits of emotional intelligence. Significantly, of the nearly 100,000 youth surveyed by Search Institute only 24% believed they experienced the asset of a caring school climate— the school provides a caring, encouraging environment.[13] Therefore, a staggering 76% do not perceive their school as supportive and enabling.

How well we resolve this collective emotional crisis will depend on our willingness and ability to formulate new and creative answers to the questions posed in this book. Trying harder with current strategies likely will yield little relief from current troubling conditions and may actually, by normalizing those conditions, contribute to our problems.

Endnotes

1. The University of Tennessee Center for Government Training, *Safe and Drug Free Life* (Knoxville, TN: Author, 1997).

2. K. S. Peterson, "1 Million School Kids Toting Guns," *USA Today*, 19 June 1998, sec. D, p. 6.

3. D. Lockwood, "Violence among Middle School and High School Students: Analysis and Implications for Prevention," *Research in Brief* (National Institute for Justice, October 1997).

4. M. J. Elias, "Preventing Youth Violence," *Education Week* 2 August (1995), 54.

5. W. DeJong, "School-Based Violence Prevention: From Peaceable School to the Peaceable Neighborhood," *National Institute for Dispute Resolution Forum* (Spring 1994), 8–14.

6. P. Moore and D. Batiste, "Preventing Youth Violence: Prejudice Elimination and Conflict Resolution Programs," *National Institute for Dispute Resolution Forum* (Spring 1994), 15–19.

7. M. Haberman and V. Schreiber Dill, "Commitment to Violence Among Teenagers in Poverty," *Kappa Delta Pi Record* (Spring 1995), 149–154.

8. M. J. Elias, J. E. Zins, R. P. Weissberg, K. S. Frey, M. T. Greenberg, N. M. Haynes, R. Kessler, M. E. Schwab-Stone, and T. P. Shriver, *Promoting Social and Emotional Learning: Guidelines for Educators* (Alexandria, VA: Association for Supervision and Curriculum Development, 1997).

9. Search Institute, *The Asset Approach: Giving Kids What They Need to Succeed* (Minneapolis: Author, 1997).

10. Search Institute, *The Asset Approach*, 2, 4.

11. D. Hamburg, *Today's Children: Creating a Future for a Generation in Crisis* (New York: Times Books, 1992), 171–172.

12. D. Goleman, *Emotional Intelligence* (New York: Bantam Books, 1995), xi–xii.

13. Search Institute, *The Asset Approach*, 2.

CHAPTER 2

Emotional Intelligence

Ramone and Nina are working on the dinosaur project in the science center. It begins, as likely do most disputes among 6-year-olds in a first-grade classroom. Everyone in the room can hear Ramone and Nina yelling at each other. Today is the day that the 15-foot papier-mâché replication of the Tyrannosaurus Rex is to be painted. In a class meeting, the class had decided what colors to paint their dinosaur, named "Rex." A chart that graphed their color choices was made for the science center. Their dinosaur was to have a brown body with lots of green sponge dots, yellow and purple eyes, black toes and nose tip, white teeth, and a magenta tongue.

Nina: *Ramone, you are not painting the tongue. Magenta was my idea, so I'm painting the tongue.*

Ramone: *You are not. I had the magenta first.*

Nina: *I'm painting the tongue. Give me the magenta. (She grabs it from him.)*

Ramone: *I had it first. (He grabs it back.)*

Nina: *You are not going to be my friend anymore.*

Ramone: *I don't want to be your friend.*

As their teacher Mrs. Washington approaches the science center, Nina throws the container of magenta paint at Ramone. Ramone begins to cry, "Mrs. Washington, I hate Nina. She ruined my new shirt, and my mama will whip me." Nina yells, "It's his fault—he took the magenta paint, and it was my idea." To Mrs. Washington, this is typical of behaviors that steal her time from teaching the reading group or working in the math center. Speaking angrily, she responds by having Ramone and Nina clean up the paint and apologize to each other. She tells Nina and Ramone that they will not be allowed to paint the dinosaur for the remainder of the week. Ramone is then sent to the school social worker to get a change of clothes so the ones covered in paint can soak in the classroom sink.

Mrs. Washington's actions are typical of the consequences used by teachers in classrooms across the country to help children learn to behave. So what is wrong with this picture? Ramone and Nina are emotionally illiterate, and this classroom experience is counter-productive to their becoming emotionally intelligent. What did the students learn from this experience? Does Ramone understand why he behaved as he did? Does Nina? Does either Ramone or Nina grasp the meaning of the other's actions? Who solved the problem? What is Ramone's and Nina's relationship? Will Mrs. Washington's handling of the incident prevent future similar incidents?

What Is Emotional Intelligence?

Quite simply, emotional intelligence is the intelligent use of emotions—intentionally making your emotions work for you by using them to help guide your behavior and thinking in ways that enhance your ability to satisfy your basic needs and to obtain your wants. Yale psychologist Peter Salovey and psychologist John Mayer of the University of New Hampshire pioneered the definition of emotional intelligence in 1990 by framing emotional abilities as crossing five domains.[1]

1. Knowing one's emotions
2. Managing emotions
3. Motivating oneself
4. Recognizing emotions in others
5. Handling relationships

Emotional intelligence derives from basic elements that, if nurtured with experience, enable an individual to develop specific skills and abilities. These skills and abilities are the building blocks of emotional intelligence. Unlike elements of one's intelligence quotient (IQ), these building blocks can be developed to allow an individual to dramatically increase emotional intelligence. The building blocks are hierarchical, with each level incorporating and building upon the capabilities of all previous levels. Specifically, the building blocks are as follows:[2]

1. The ability to accurately perceive, appraise, and express emotion

2. The ability to access or generate feelings on demand when they can facilitate understanding of self or another

3. The ability to understand emotions and the knowledge that derives from them

4. The ability to regulate emotions to promote emotional and intellectual growth

Each of the domains of emotional intelligence has major implications for learning and thus for teaching. Emotions play an enormous role in what we do in school. Is it not logical that we pursue the development of emotional intelligence in our schools?

Knowing One's Emotions

Knowing one's emotions is about self-awareness, the ability to recognize a feeling as it happens. Self-awareness is what keeps us from overreacting and amplifying what is perceived. It is a detached, self-reflective state that exists even amidst highly emotional events. Self-awareness is being aware of both our emotions and our thoughts about the emotion. Being aware of our feelings and our behavior, as well as others' perceptions of us, can influence our actions so they work to our benefit. Daniel Goleman explains that people have distinctive styles for attending to and dealing with their emotions.

> *Self-aware.* Aware of their moods as they are having them, these people understandably have some sophistication about their emotional lives. Their clarity about emotions may undergird other personality traits: they are autonomous and sure of their own boundaries, are in good psychological health, and tend to have a positive outlook on life. When they get into a bad mood, they don't ruminate and obsess about it, and are able to get out of it sooner. In short, their mindfulness helps them manage their emotions.

Engulfed. These are people who often feel swamped by their emotions and helpless to escape them, as though their moods have taken charge. They are mercurial and not very aware of their feelings, so that they are lost in them rather than having some perspective. As a result, they do little to try to escape bad moods, feeling that they have no control over their emotional life. They feel overwhelmed and emotionally out of control.

Accepting. While these people are often clear about what they are feeling, they also tend to be accepting of their moods, and so don't try to change them. There seem to be two branches of the accepting type: those who are usually in good moods and so have little motivation to change them, and people who, despite their clarity about their moods, are susceptible to bad ones but accept them with a laissez-faire attitude, doing nothing to change them despite their distress—a pattern found among, say, depressed people who are resigned to their despair.[3]

It is important to realize that style is not destiny. Individuals are malleable and can learn self-awareness. Specifically, those with predominately engulfed and accepting emotional styles can learn self-awareness. Self-awareness is fundamental to psychological insight. There are two levels of emotion, conscious and unconscious. Any emotion can be, and often is, unconscious. When emotions simmer beneath the threshold of our awareness they can have a powerful impact upon how we perceive and how we react, even though we have no idea they are at work. It is only when the emotion is brought into awareness that the individual has the ability to choose behavior. Once awareness registers, one can evaluate, examine options, and choose a reaction. Emotional self-awareness is thus the cornerstone of emotional intelligence, serving as the building block for the other fundamentals of emotional intelligence.

Emotional intelligence can only begin when affective information enters the perceptual system. High self-awareness enables you to monitor yourself, to observe yourself in action. You need to understand what is important to you, how you experience things, what you want and why you want what you want, how you feel, and how others perceive you. This subjective knowledge about the nature of your personality not only guides your behavior from situation to situation, it provides you with a solid framework for making better choices.

Managing Emotions

Perhaps you have been admonished or have admonished someone else to "get in control of your emotions" or "chill out." This is often interpreted to mean "stifle your emotions." Managing emotions is about balance, not emotional suppression. Our emotions provide us with lots of clues as to why we do what we do, and stifling them deprives us of that information. Suppressing emotions also does not make them go away; suppression can leave emotions free to fester, as is often the case with anger. The goal is appropriate feelings proportionate to circumstance. When emotions are too flat, they yield numbness, apathy, indifference, or disconnectedness. However, emotions that are continually intense and out of control develop into depression, extreme anxiety, or raging anger. Balancing intense emotions is the key to emotional well being. As Goleman points out, managing our emotions is something of a full-time job. Much of what we do—especially in our free time—is an attempt to manage mood. Reading a novel, watching television, and choosing certain activities and companions all can be ways to make ourselves feel better. Managing emotions is understanding them and then using that understanding to turn situations to our benefit, to create situations that are need satisfying.

Learning skills for dealing with moods such as anger, anxiety, and sadness helps individuals develop resiliency—the ability to bounce back from the challenges of life. Developing anger management skills is a potent way to defuse anger so we become more effective at dealing with the problem that triggered the anger in the first place. Recent research suggests that anger is a secondary emotion—that is, another strong feeling precedes the anger: fear, worry, hurt, inadequacy, or the perception of being in the one-down position (having less power, influence, resources, or control than others). This understanding can help us identify anger triggers at an early stage. Also, anger often operates "out of time"—that is, the anger is an echo from a past time and not triggered by a present phenomenon. Learning to utilize relaxation methods, to reframe a situation, to change perspectives, and to write down hostile thoughts and reappraise them are proven methods for managing anger. Early identification of feelings associated with fears, worries, and notions of disadvantage can avert angry outbursts.

Developing skills for dealing with anxiety means learning effective ways to deal with worrisome thoughts before they lead to insomnia and anxiety disorders such as phobias and obsessions. Learning to identify worries at an early point in the anxiety spiral, applying relaxation methods, and then actively challenging the worrisome thoughts is a process for breaking the worrying habit.

A key concept in managing sadness is that bereavement is useful, whereas depression is not. The sadness associated with a loss for a period of time typically closes down interests, fixates attention on what is lost, absorbs energy for new endeavors. This mourning or bereavement period is time to reflect on the meaning of the loss and make the psychological adjustments and plans that will allow life to continue. Depression, on the other hand, involves self-hatred, a sense of worthlessness, gloom, dread, alienation, failure of mental focus, and loss of pleasure and hope. Depression can range from mild to major. Developing skills for managing sadness is focused on the range of depression that people can handle on their own if they have the internal resources. Sadness experienced as ordinary melancholy is within the range of despondency that the individual can handle on his or her own if that person possesses the internal resources of emotional intelligence. Without those resources, sadness often escalates to more severe, often debilitating depression. Goleman suggests that one of the main determinants of whether a depressed mood will persist or lift is the degree to which people ruminate. Worrying about what is depressing us makes the depression all the more intense and prolonged. In depression, worry takes several forms, all focusing on some aspect of the depression itself—for instance, how tired we feel, how little energy or motivation we have, or how little work we are getting done. Typically, none of this reflection is accompanied by any concrete course of action that might alleviate the problem. Passive immersion in the sadness simply makes it worse. Learning to challenge the thoughts at the center of rumination and to schedule enjoyable activities, particularly with others, are effective methods for dealing with mild depression.

In major depression, life is paralyzed, without new beginnings. Major depression requires professional treatment.

Emotional distress can have a devastating impact on mental clarity. The emotional brain at times seems to overpower, even paralyze the thinking brain. Goleman points out that the extent to which emotional upsets can interfere with mental life is not new to educators: "Students who are anxious, angry or depressed don't learn; people who are caught in these states do not take in information efficiently or deal with it well. . . . When emotions overwhelm concentration, what is being swamped is the mental capacity cognitive scientists call 'working memory', the ability to hold in mind all information relevant to the task at hand."[4] Without the ability to manage them, powerful negative emotions overwhelm thoughts and abilities, rendering one unable to take appropriate action to cope successfully with life problems. Findings reported by Goleman from a massive survey of parents and teachers suggest there is a worldwide trend in this present generation of children to be more troubled emotionally than prior generations. Is it little wonder, then, that test scores are declining? Considering the impact of emotional distress on mental clarity, is focusing on only the cognitive dimension of learning likely to reverse this decline?

Although the emotions generally thought to be negative—anger, anxiety, fear, depression, frustration—are usually the focus, positive emotions such as joy, enthusiasm, contentment, and confidence also require skilled management. Enthusiasm or confidence, for example, may cause one to agree to take on more than can be handled. Contentment may result in reduced motivation. Especially in social contexts, joy or confidence may be viewed suspiciously by others.

Motivating Oneself

Motivation is expending energy in a specific direction for a specific purpose. Being emotionally intelligent, in the context of motivation, means using your emotional system to catalyze the whole process and keep the process of expending energy going. Self-motivation is about self-responsibility. Goleman speaks about self-motivation as the ability to channel emotions toward a productive end: "Whether it be in controlling impulse and putting off gratification, regulating our moods so they facilitate rather than impede thinking, motivating ourselves to persist and try, try again in the face of setbacks, or finding ways to enter flow and so perform more effectively—all bespeak the power of emotion to guide effective effort."[5] To some degree, emotions either get in the way of or enhance our ability to think and plan, to pursue training for a distant goal, and to solve problems. How we do in life is determined largely by the degree to which we take responsibility for our emotions. Emotions define the limits of our capacity to use our innate mental abilities. When we are motivated by feelings of enthusiasm and pleasure in what we do—or even by an optimal degree of anxiety—emotions propel us to accomplishment: "It is in this sense that emotional intelligence is a master aptitude, a capacity that profoundly affects all other abilities, either facilitating or interfering with them."[6]

A fundamental psychological skill, at the root of all emotional self-control, is impulse control. Resisting impulse or delaying gratification is the root of all emotional self-control, since all emotions, by their very nature, lead to one or another impulse to act. Learning to deny one's impulses or delay gratification in order to achieve a goal or long-term benefit is a skill that can have a profound impact on social-emotional competence in life. It is the very essence of emotional self-regulation. Can school interventions be designed to foster impulse control in those who appear to lack the ability to delay gratification, as well as to enhance this essential psychological skill in those who already exhibit an inclination to delay gratification for possible future gain?

Learning to manage moods has intellectual benefits. Goleman explains that good moods, while they last, enhance the ability to think flexibly and with more complexity, thus making it easier to find solutions to problems, whether intellectual or interpersonal:

> Laughing, like elation, seems to help people think more broadly and associate more freely, noticing relationships that might have eluded them otherwise—a mental skill important not just in creativity, but in recognizing complex relationships and foreseeing the consequences of a

given decision. . . . Even mild mood changes can sway thinking. In making plans or decisions people in good moods have a perceptual bias that leads them to be more expansive and positive in their thinking.[7]

Emotions out of control impede our ability to think in positive ways, thus squelching the motivation provided by hope and optimism.

Hope plays a potent role in life, offering advantages in school and life achievement. Hope is the internal confidence that you can summon the will and means to accomplish your goals. Self-motivation is a trait found in people with high levels of hope. Hopeful people feel resourceful in finding ways to accomplish their objectives, reassure themselves when in a rough situation that things will get better, are flexible in finding different ways to get to their goals or to switch goals if one becomes impossible, and have the sense to break down an overwhelming task into smaller, more manageable segments. Hope is a key attribute of the emotionally intelligent. Hope makes it possible for one not to give in to overwhelming anxiety or succumb to depression or develop a defeatist attitude when faced with difficult challenges or even setbacks. Individuals who possess a success identity likely have the quality of hope as a well-developed trait. They are optimists.

Like hope, optimism means having a strong expectation that things will turn out all right in life, despite setbacks and frustrations. Optimism is an attitude that protects people from falling into apathy, hopelessness, or depression in the face of challenging and difficult life experiences. Optimists view failure as due to something that can be changed in order to succeed in the future. They have a "success identity." Even though they may not always succeed, they do accept responsibility for their actions and results. Pessimists blame themselves for failure due to some permanent characteristic that they cannot change. Pessimism induces apathy, defeatism, and despair. Pessimists, even when successful, attribute their good fortune to circumstances removed from them, such as being in the right place at the right time, knowing the right persons, being lucky, and so forth. They have a "failure identity." Although they may not always fail, they tend not to accept responsibility for their actions and results. Optimism incites hope. Goleman explains that

> optimism and hope—like helplessness and despair—can be learned. Underlying both is an outlook psychologists call self-efficacy, the belief that one has mastery over the events of one's life and can meet challenges as they arise. Developing a competency of any kind strengthens the sense of self-efficacy, making a person more willing to take risks and seek out more demanding challenges. Surmounting those challenges in turn increases the sense of self-efficacy. This attitude makes people more likely to make the best use of whatever skills they may have—or to do what it takes to develop them.[8]

Self-efficacy helps people bounce back from failures. Individuals who have a sense of efficacy approach failure as a learning experience and look for the growth opportunities in the process.

Another way people self-motivate is through the intrinsically rewarding experience of what Mihaly Csikszentmihalyi, a University of Chicago psychologist, defines as *flow*.[9] Flow is a state in which people become utterly absorbed in what they are doing, paying undivided attention to the task, losing track of time and space. Flow is marked by feelings of spontaneous joy. When people are in flow they are so engrossed in the task at hand that they lose all self-consciousness. It is the pleasure of the task that motivates them. In flow, it is impossible to ruminate and worry. The ability to enter flow is the ultimate in emotional intelligence. When in flow the emotions are energized and aligned with the task at hand—the emotions are at a positive peak. Flow is much more than simply containing and channeling emotions. Containing and channeling emotions are important to emotional intelligence but do not equate to flow. Further, negative emotions such as fear, anxiety, or depression block flow.

Flow is about internal motivation rather than external motivation by threat of punishment or promise of reward. Individuals, including children, learn best when they care about something and when they are engaged in a pursuit that gives them pleasure.

Can a school environment be created so that flow becomes a common experience in schools? Can students experience flow in the learning experiences we design for them? Is learning likely without flow? Independent learners likely experience flow frequently.

Recognizing Emotions in Others

Recognizing emotions in others is *empathy*. Empathy is the ability to read and grasp the emotions of another person. Goleman states, "People's emotions are rarely put into words; far more often they are expressed through other cues. The key to intuiting another's feelings is in the ability to read nonverbal channels: tone of voice, gesture, facial expression, and the like."[10] Children learn empathy by seeing how others react when distressed and then imitating what they see. They learn empathy when discipline for misbehavior requires them to focus attention on the distress their behavior has caused someone else. Children learn empathy by having their feelings understood and shared by another. If their emotions are not met with empathy, accepted, and reciprocated, children will not learn how to attune to the feelings of another. When they do not receive empathy for feelings such as joy or sorrow, they eventually avoid expressing and sometimes even feeling those emotions.

Empathy has a profound link to ethics and moral development. If people cannot empathize with others—experience their pain, danger, or deprivation—they will not be able to act to help them. Empathy gives us the ability to put oneself in another's place and to make informed decisions. It is developmentally appropriate to expect advanced levels of empathy to emerge by late childhood. By that stage of development, young people can understand distress beyond the immediate situation. They are capable of understanding that one's life circumstances—poverty, oppression, exclusion, and so forth—may be a source of chronic, often immobilizing, distress. Adolescents can empathize with an entire group—for example, the poor or the disabled or the exploited—and often can mobilize their moral convictions into action campaigns designed to alleviate injustice or misfortune. This developmental time frame indicates that empathy evolvement is a legitimate issue for schools to address.

Can a sense of community that fosters empathy be created not just in a classroom here or there but throughout a school? Is empathy a likely outcome if the community is characterized by competition for scarce resources?

Handling Relationships

Emotional skills are essential for the preservation of relationships, whether the relationship is with others of similar age or with individuals either younger or older, whether the relationship is a friendship or a partnership for some purpose other than friendship. Goleman says,

> Those who are adept in social intelligence can connect with people quite smoothly, be astute in reading their reactions and feelings, lead and organize, and handle the disputes that are bound to flare up in any human activity. They are the natural leaders, the people who can express the unspoken collective sentiment and articulate it so as to guide a group toward its goals. They are the kind of people others like to be with because they are emotionally nourishing—they leave other people in a good mood.[11]

These interpersonal abilities, however, must be balanced by an astute sense of one's own needs and feelings and how to fulfill them. Crucial to emotional competence is the capacity to be true to oneself and act in accord with one's deepest feelings and values no matter what the emotional consequences.

The basis of any relationship is communication. Without communication there is no connection and hence no relationship. The skills of effective and productive communication assure that exchanges within relationships have the greatest chance for positive outcomes. These skills include the following:

- Self-disclosure: Telling the other person what you think, feel, want, need

- Assertiveness: Standing up for your opinions, ideas, beliefs, and needs while respecting those of others

- Listening: Hearing the other person's verbal and non-verbal messages to determine what that person is really saying
- Facilitating: Enabling the other person to deliver a complete message; delivering your message in a manner that maximizes the other person's ability to hear you

Sensitivity is a trait of the emotionally intelligent individual that ensures effective communication. Interpersonal effectiveness also requires the skills of cooperation and conflict resolution. People without the skills of cooperation and conflict resolution suffer constantly in the sense that their needs continually go unfulfilled and their relationships are unstable and unsatisfying. In short, without these skills such individuals are constantly at the mercy of their circumstances or, more accurately, at the mercy of others.

Developing Emotional Intelligence

The scene between Ramone and Nina described at the beginning of this chapter need not be typical. With instruction for emotional skill development and a system for classroom management that facilitates emotional development, children like Ramone and Nina can learn to be emotionally intelligent. They also can learn to use that emerging intelligence to employ processes of constructive conflict resolution. The following scenario illustrates how Ramone and Nina might respond to their problem differently, with emotional intelligence.

Nina:	*Ramone, you are not painting the tongue. Magenta was my idea, so I'm painting the tongue.*
Ramone:	*You are not. I had the magenta first.*
Nina:	*I'm painting the tongue. Give me the magenta. (She grabs it from him.)*
Ramone:	*I had it first. (He grabs it back.)*
Mrs. Washington:	*Nina, Ramone, could the two of you cool off and then choose ways to problem solve?*

Nina:	*What? I guess so.*
Ramone:	*Yes, probably.*
Mrs. Washington:	*Can you do it now? Can you go to the peace corner and talk it out?*
Ramone:	*OK! Nina, let's go to the corner.*
Nina:	*I want to talk first. OK?*
Ramone:	*Go ahead.*
Nina:	*Ramone, I really want to paint the tongue magenta because it was my idea. I am mad at you because you have already started painting it. Did you hear me say that I was going to do it at our class meeting?*
Ramone:	*No, I didn't know that you wanted to paint the tongue magenta just because it was your idea. I want to paint the tongue magenta, too. I know you are mad at me.*
Nina:	*OK! We both want to paint the tongue magenta, and there is only one brush for magenta. That's the problem.*
Ramone:	*I guess we have a conflict. Do you want to negotiate, or should we get a peer mediator to help us solve this problem?*
Nina:	*I think we can talk it out by ourselves. What do you think?*
Ramone:	*OK, let's try. I agree to take turns talking and listening, and I agree to cooperate to solve this problem.*
Nina:	*I agree to take turns talking and listening, and I agree to cooperate with you to solve this problem.*
Ramone:	*My point of view is that I don't like it when you yell at me. This dinosaur thing is a class project, and I want to work on it. Mrs. Washington said I could paint*

	now, and she didn't say anything about not painting the tongue. I like magenta. I was here first, so maybe you should choose something else to paint.
Nina:	*I'm sorry I yelled at you, but I was pretty upset. I had been thinking about painting the tongue all morning. You say it was your turn to paint, and Mrs. Washington didn't tell you not to paint the tongue. You chose the tongue because you like the color the class decided upon. Well, I thought up the idea of painting the tongue magenta, so I think I should be allowed to paint it. I think this special choice of tongue color is what will make the dinosaur so neat. You didn't think up any color ideas, so if you want to paint, just paint something else. It's a great big animal.*
Ramone:	*You think because it was your idea to have the tongue be magenta that you should get to paint it. You think that this color on the tongue will make this dinosaur really neat, and you want others to know it was your idea. I'm not sure that's fair, but I can see it is important to you. I started painting the tongue because it is a small part and I'm a good, neat painter. I wanted the dinosaur to look good. Besides, I'm almost finished.*
Nina:	*So you want the dinosaur to look good, and you think you paint well. What do you think we should do?*
Ramone:	*You could let me finish painting the tongue, and then we could make a sign that says the tongue color was Nina's idea and Ramone painted it.*

Nina:	You could give me the magenta brush and let me finish the tongue, and then we could choose to paint something else together where there's two brushes for that color.
Ramone:	We could ask Mrs. Washington to have a class meeting and have people sign up to paint certain parts. That could keep others from having a problem like this one.
Nina:	I think I should apologize for yelling at you. I was upset and didn't think. Next time I'll try to talk calmly.
Ramone:	Maybe we can both try talking instead of yelling. Friends shouldn't yell at each other.
Nina:	I think the sign is a good idea and asking Mrs. Washington to assign painters would probably help this project.
Ramone:	I think I could let you finish the tongue if you want to. I'd like us to do something together also.
Nina:	I'm sorry I yelled at you. I'm going to tell Mrs. Washington we worked it out. I'll tell her I'm sorry also and that you didn't really do anything wrong.
Ramone:	I think this is worked out. Are we friends again?

Realistically, very few children, probably very few adults, could carry on such a dialog at the mere prompting of a third party. Nearly all persons, children and adults, can learn to problem solve in this manner. However, opportunities to develop the foundation abilities of conflict resolution—orientation, perception, emotion, communication, creative thinking, and critical thinking—are required. With abilities developed or developing, individuals can learn conflict resolution processes, then resolve conflicts nonviolently and civilly.

The development of the orientation abilities is crucial because possessing the view that problems are opportunities and having the inclination to want to work things out is the contrivance that triggers the process into action. Even when students are trained in conflict resolution, one very important service adults continue to provide is to call students' attention to opportunities to use their training, just as Mrs. Washington did for Nina and Ramone.

The foundation abilities of perception, emotion, and communication are the heart of emotional intelligence. The creative and critical thinking abilities allow for the employment of emotional intelligence in interpersonal interactions. The processes of conflict resolution allow the emotionally intelligent person to invent and develop lasting resolutions to interpersonal problems between individuals and between and among groups of individuals. These abilities can be developed in our children in our schools. Doing so requires the effort, not just the intention. It makes sense to use children's current behavior as their subject matter to learn to be emotionally intelligent. Adults can facilitate a learning laboratory that develops the capacity of children to behave in emotionally intelligent ways. To do so, the adults must create a culture of encouragement and capacity building. This will mean abandoning the predominant culture of schools, as well as the culture of most other places in which children and adults coexist, where children are simply judged on their ability to behave or not behave appropriately.

Endnotes

1. P. Salovey and J. Mayer, "Emotional Intelligence," *Imagination, Cognition, and Personality 9* (1990), 189.

2. H. Weisinger, *Emotional Intelligence at Work* (San Francisco: Jossey-Bass, 1998), xvii–xviii.

3. Daniel Goleman, *Emotional Intelligence* (New York: Bantam Books, 1995), 48.

4. Goleman, *Emotional Intelligence,* 78–79.

5. Goleman, *Emotional Intelligence,* 95.

6. Goleman, *Emotional Intelligence,* 80.

7. Goleman, *Emotional Intelligence,* 85.

8. Goleman, *Emotional Intelligence*, 89–90.

9. M. Csikszentmihalyi, *Flow: The Psychology of Optimal Experience* (New York: Harper and Row, 1990), 4.

10. Goleman, *Emotional Intelligence*, 96.

11. Goleman, *Emotional Intelligence*, 118–119.

CHAPTER 3

Classroom Barriers to Emotional Development

It seems that nearly everyone wants to improve schooling in the United States, but there seems to be little consensus on the form that improvement should take. Some champion the point of view that schools should strengthen basic skills; others, critical thinking. Some support the point of view that schools should promote citizenship or character; others want schools to warn against the dangers of drugs and violence. Still other points of view call for schools to demand more of parents, or to accent the role of community, or to emphasize core values, or to focus on respecting diversity and promoting multiculturalism. Even those who appear to want the same reforms in schools often promote very different ways to achieve those particular reforms. Even though these points of view differ dramatically, all seemingly recognize that schools do play an essential role in preparing our young people to become knowledgeable, responsible, caring adults.

Knowledgeable. Responsible. Caring. Behind each concept lies educational challenge. For youth to become knowledgeable, they must be ready and motivated to learn, and capable of integrating new information into their lives. For youth to become responsible, they must be able to understand risks and opportunities, and be motivated to choose actions and behaviors that serve not only their own interests but also those of others. For youth to become caring, they must be able to see beyond themselves and appreciate the concerns of others; they must believe that to care is to be part of a community that is welcoming, nurturing, and concerned about them.

In the Association for Supervision and Curriculum Development's publication *Promoting Social and Emotional Learning: Guidelines for Educators,* the authors state that the challenge of raising knowledgeable, responsible and caring children is recognized by nearly everyone. Few realize, however, that each element of this challenge can be enhanced by thoughtful, sustained, and systematic attention to children's social and emotional learning. Indeed, experience and research show that promoting social and emotional development in children is the missing piece in efforts to reach the array of goals associated with improving schooling in the United States.[1]

Although collectively school personnel see the importance of programs to enhance students' social, emotional, and physical well-being, educators often also regard prevention campaigns with skepticism and frustration because most of these reform measures have been introduced as disjointed fads or a series of "wars" against one problem or another. Although well intentioned, these efforts have achieved limited success due to a lack of coordinated strategy.[2] Furthermore, backlash to the perceived limited success or downright failure of these reform efforts often creates a system less responsive to the social-emotional needs of the participants.

Acting on the choice to actively promote the development of emotional intelligence in our schools involves a great deal more than constructing and delivering specific lessons on anger management, character development, values formation, compassion, and so on. The issue is not just one of curriculum—different classes or new lessons to be added to an already crowded agenda. Barriers to the development of emotional intelligence permeate the structures of schools and thus the structures of classrooms. Changing teaching intents without making the systemic changes necessary to allow those intents to succeed will not produce the desired results. Systemic change is necessary in any program directed toward development of emotional intelligence for that development to be integral to, and not adjunct to, the classroom and the school. Systems thinking is required to design and implement changes at the level that will actually facilitate a classroom's reaching the goal of developing responsible learners through emotional intelligence.

The Peaceable Classroom

Kreidler (1984) defines the peaceable classroom as a classroom that is a warm and caring community, where there are five qualities present:

1. Cooperation. Children learn to work together and trust, help, and share with each other.

2. Communication. Children learn to observe carefully, communicate accurately, and listen sensitively.

3. Tolerance. Children learn to respect and appreciate people's differences and to understand prejudice and how it works.

4. Positive emotional expression. Children learn to express feelings, particularly anger and frustration, in ways that are not aggressive or destructive, and children learn self-control.

5. Conflict resolution. Children learn the skills of responding creatively to conflict in the context of a supportive, caring community.[3]

Any classroom with these five qualities would certainly be an environment that would support the development of emotional intelligence. Likely, every teacher wants these five qualities to exist in his or her classroom. Few classrooms, however, are peaceable classrooms. Classroom observations reveal contrasts like those described in chapter 1, where a classroom generally judged as "good" shares many characteristics with those that appear to be largely dysfunctional. Instead of cooperation, classrooms are typified by a culture of competition. Students pervasively compete for scarce rewards such as grades, privileges, or adult attention and approval. Cooperative learning opportunities are rare. Students are not regularly expected to help other students. How can the system be changed so cooperation becomes the operative value? Can the balance between competition and cooperation be tipped toward cooperation—not just to allow students to be nice to each other, but to enable them to accomplish higher goals?

In most classrooms, communication is largely one-directional, rarely concise and clear, and seldom encourages further substantive exchange. Typically, the teacher talks, and the students may or may not listen. The teacher rarely checks, at the moment of the communication, to determine what the student or students actually heard. The student talks, and the teacher listens only when the student speaks in a manner the teacher finds acceptable—perceived by the teacher as respectful—and talks about what the teacher is interested in promoting. Even then, there is rarely feedback or constructive challenge, almost never summation. Students rarely talk to one another about the content of the teaching. Can learning to be an effective verbal communicator receive at least as much attention as learning to read and write? Is verbal communication not more pivotal to interpersonal endeavors than either reading or writing? What can be changed to encourage, even demand, increased competence in interpersonal communication?

Instead of tolerance, the classroom promotes the Western, white, middle-class culture and diminishes all others—if not intentionally, then certainly by omission. The curriculum is rarely consistently multicultural. The behavioral expectations are culturally and gender biased. Is it possible for schools actually to be what is hoped for in our larger society? Could we actually move beyond tolerance to genuine appreciation of differences?

Instead of learning self-control, students must determine how to please the adult authority in order to avoid the punishments and/or reap the rewards controlled by that authority. This behavior is extrinsically driven. Can schools become the institution that finally legitimatizes emotions as an important—no, necessary—part of the human condition? Can educators actually embrace emotions as content for learning, accepting the notion that understanding and managing this domain of the human condition is at least as important as doing so for the cognitive domain?

Instead of conflict resolution processes that allow those in conflict to problem solve constructively, the system appears to view conflict as unnatural, certainly unwanted. Even arguments over the content of learning are unwelcome. The only thing worse than conflict between students arguing with each other is the kind where the student has the temerity to challenge the teacher. Disputes that do surface are settled by an adult arbitrator or, more frequently, disputing students are advised to avoid each other or the problem situation. Is it possible to have an institutional expectation that conflict is natural but each has a responsibility to seek resolutions that meet the needs of all? Can practicing peace—honoring oneself, honoring others, honoring the environment—be the behavioral expectation for all who participate in the system, children and adults?

Organizations, like individuals, choose to handle conflicts in negative or positive ways. In organizations as with individuals, how conflicts are managed and not their presence determines if the outcomes are destructive or constructive. For students to learn and practice conflict resolution, it is important for the school to be *conflict positive*. As David W. Johnson and Roger T. Johnson of the University of Minnesota's Conflict Resolution and Cooperative Learning Center note, "Conflict positive schools manage conflicts constructively to enhance the quality of teaching, learning, and school life. They recognize that conflicts are inevitable, healthy, and valuable. Conflicts are not problems—they are part of solutions."[4] Conflict positive schools recognize that conflicts are natural and do not occur just between students, but occur between and among all segments of the school population. To be a conflict-positive school requires that a critical mass of adults and students be trained to use, and regularly use, conflict resolution strategies. Such a school recognizes that the behavior of the adults in the school sends students the most powerful message about behavioral expectations. If the expectation is for students to manage and resolve conflicts constructively, students must observe adults consistently behaving in a like manner. A conflict-positive school promotes academic controversy. Using conflict in academic lessons makes operational the belief that conflict is opportunity and often the foundation for growth—individual and societal. Can schools be reconstituted as conflict-positive systems? Is not the ultimate mission of our schools to prepare our youth to be future contributing participators in our democratic processes?

H. Jerome Freiberg asserts that although we teach about democracy, we rarely practice it in our schools and classrooms.[5] He goes on to say that creating caring classrooms and supportive schools will improve opportunities for students to become citizens rather than tourists. Tourists simply pass through without involvement, commitment, or belonging. In places where people respect them and care about them as individuals, students can learn to become informed and involved members of our democratic society. To turn tourists into citizens, educators need to create active classrooms, where cooperation, participation, and support are fundamental. Such a classroom is neither totally teacher centered nor totally student centered: It is person centered. In contrast, most classrooms rely heavily on teacher control and student obedience. Reliance on teacher or other adult control appears to correlate strongly with the perceived difficulty of the student population; thus, inner city schools and schools with substantial minority or at-risk populations are very often the most controlling. In many of these classrooms, there appears to be a tacit operational agreement between students and teacher: "Leave me alone, and I won't give you trouble." Therefore, student populations often judged to be the most lacking in emotional intelligence are those subjected to the most controlling management, the very strategy one would use to create tourists in a hurry to leave.

It does not have to be this way. Three ways schools can prepare youth to live productively in a democratic society are to provide safe, socially just, and cooperative learning environments. These goals include achievement of the following:

- An environment in which each person feels physically and psychologically free from threats and danger, not just from students but also from adults

- An arena in which adults as well as students can find opportunities to work and learn together to the mutual enhancement of all

- An environment in which students and adults respect, cherish, enhance, and celebrate the diversity of its population

- An arena that provides students and adults equal access and opportunity free from consideration of race, ethnicity, religion, culture, gender, sexual orientation, physical and mental abilities, or social class[6]

Classrooms and schools are what they are because they strive to meet the system's expectations. Any classroom and any school likely could, with expanded resources and/or more concerted effort,

better meet those expectations. Doing so, however, will not eliminate or likely even diminish the problems that nearly everyone iden-
tifies as issues central to our educational crisis. Determining how
better to meet existing expectations is approaching the problem
nonsystemically. Classrooms and schools are not peaceable precisely because they DO meet system expectations, not because they
DO NOT meet those expectations.

Punishments and Rewards

Consider the problem of children's not behaving responsibly in
school. Symptoms of this problem typically include defiance, bul-
lying, verbal and physical confrontations, little engagement in
learning, incomplete homework, and the like. Approaching this
problem nonsystemically, we apply symptomatic solutions—solutions designed to ameliorate the symptoms. Punishments and
rewards are the most common symptomatic solutions to the problem of children's not behaving responsibly or, more accurately, not
behaving compliantly, in school. Punishment is often applied in
the form of suspensions, detentions, threats of failing grades, additional assignments, or withholding attention. The idea is that if
children find the consequences distasteful or, more aptly, fear the
consequences, they will alter their future behavior. But what do
children today actually fear? Schools regularly deal with children
who have suffered abuses far more severe than anything schools
can or would, in good conscience, devise as punishments.

Some educators recognize that punishment may not be an
effective strategy, or at least that it is an unpleasant practice: As a
substitute, rewards such as stickers, stars, good grades, awards,
praise, and privileges are routinely used to induce children to engage
in learning, be nice to others, and comply with adult demands.
Apparently, the thinking is that there are good ways and bad ways
to coerce students: The bad ways, harsh, mean, and cruel; the good
ways, gentle, subtle, and kindly. As with punishment, the offer
of rewards can elicit temporary compliance, making the problem
seem better for a while. Unfortunately, rewards turn out to be no
more effective than punishments in helping children learn to
become caring, responsible people or lifelong, self-directed learners. Punishments and rewards are both "low leverage" solutions;

they are not opposite sides of the coin, but rather two faces of the same side. In the long term, they rupture important relationships between adults and children as well as among children, and they are counterproductive in helping children become ethical, compassionate, critical thinkers and decision makers. Alfie Kohn suggests that punishment actually impedes the process of ethical development.[7] Ethical sophistication consists of some blend of principles and caring, of knowing how one ought to act and being concerned about others. Punishment does absolutely nothing to promote either of these things. In fact, it tends to undermine good values by fostering a preoccupation with self-interest. What consequence will I suffer for having done something bad? is a question that suggests a disturbingly primitive level of moral development, yet it is our use of punishment that keeps students from progressing beyond it. In the real world, getting children to focus on what will happen to them if they are caught misbehaving is simply not an effective way to prevent future misbehavior because it does nothing to instill a lasting commitment to better values or an inclination to attend to other's needs. Kohn goes on to assert that "rewards . . . are just 'control through seduction' . . . control of any variety is aversive and we should expect that, ultimately, rewards wouldn't work much better than punishments."[8]

Further, relying on punishments and rewards to control behavior reinforces further reliance on this type of control because these extrinsic controls override the intrinsic value of learning and behaving responsibly. Whenever things go wrong in such discipline programs—which is often—the approach itself is rarely blamed. It is the students who are said to be incorrigible or the teachers who are faulted for being insufficiently firm or skillful. Critics cite observed or reported misbehavior and clamor for more discipline. The more behavior management programs disappoint, the more they create their own demand. This is a classic example of thinking nonsystemically.

Also, reliance on punishments and rewards plays directly into the limited view of many youth that the adult's job in schools is to "make me learn" and "make me behave." Avoiding punishment or gaining a reward becomes the goal, replacing interest in learning and behaving. In school, this reliance on punishment and rewards typically results in the employment of more support staff to control student behavior, the generation of more and more rules to enforce, and the dependence on more and more detentions, suspensions, even expulsions, to solve the behavior problems. In the long term, the overall health of the school gradually worsens, and there are growing feelings of helplessness among those in the environment. Children continue to question, What do they want me to do, and what happens to me if I don't do it? or What do they want me to do, and what do I get for doing it? Both punishments and rewards focus the concern of the behaving or misbehaving individual on external factors.

Shifting the focus to structures and fundamental solutions—a strategy that leads to enduring improvement—prompts different questions to direct a course of action. Instead of asking, How motivated are the students? systems thinking asks, How are the students motivated? Instead of asking, How can students be persuaded to do what is expected? systems thinking asks, Why are students not behaving as expected? Instead of focusing on the student's meeting the curricular and behavioral expectations of school, systems thinking focuses on helping students become enthusiastic, lifelong learners and contributing members of a democratic society. From the educator's systems-thinking perspective the question becomes, How do we create a caring community of learners who are responsible decision makers? From the student's perspective the question becomes, What do I need and how can I meet my needs without denying similar opportunity to others? In the long term, the questions become, What kind of community do we want to create? and What kind of person do I want to be?

Thus, promoting the development of emotional intelligence in our classrooms and schools requires more than a curriculum for social and emotional learning. It is imperative that the system be exorcised of those expectations that work counter to the development of emotional intelligence and be designed to allow youth to learn and practice responsible citizenship through choice, not coercion. It seems logical that these systems-thinking efforts should focus on the behavior management program. Classrooms and schools cannot exist without behavior management. Can behavior management be formulated, organized, and practiced in a way that fosters responsible citizens rather than compliant ones? We believe that the development of emotional intelligence can and should be the outcome of the behavior management program. Since children do behave—that is, make behavioral choices—and since the system must manage the behavior of masses of children, practicing responsible choice making in a supportive environment is the perfect vehicle for promoting social-emotional learning. Such an approach is relevant to all. It serves management's need for social order, and it allows individuals to learn to make choices that satisfy their own needs but that are acceptable in the social context—their choices do not deprive or deny others' choices. The resulting environment will be fun and rewarding for all—adults and youths—also a basic psychological need of all. Can rigor and fun coexist? Why not? Does real learning not require rigor and is learning not fun, powerful, and freeing?

Presently, educators report spending "too much time disciplining" students who do not respect authority, do not listen, do not work, and constantly make life difficult for others. Not only are suspensions up, but educators report a dramatic increase in the number of students suspended more than once in the same school year. In addition, this growing number of students who are being repeatedly suspended for misbehavior are mostly students in elementary and middle school rather than high school. These are troubling trends that support the need to manage schools more effectively. Educators are often discouraged by the notion that change is impossible without total social reforms to end problems such as poverty, racism, and drug abuse. The difficulty with this thinking is that it can justify inaction when there are interventions that can make a significant difference in breaking the cycles of violent, self-destructive, disruptive, irresponsible behavior.

It seems obvious that detentions and suspensions are ineffective but overused. These practices do not alter behavior and directly contradict the support of students' psychological needs for belonging, respect, and empowerment. Little wonder many youth in schools today are detached from the adults who work with them and from the institution itself. An assistant principal who works mostly with discipline concerns in a middle school summarized these issues eloquently at a workshop we conducted: "We are trying to solve today's problems with yesterday's solutions—and it is not working."

While youth are particularly vulnerable to complex societal problems, they are also resilient and reachable. Researchers in the area of resiliency have consistently shown that the single most important factor in fostering resiliency in students, especially those students who are at risk, is the development of a positive relationship with a caring adult. Teachers, administrators, school counselors, social workers, deans, psychologists, and so forth are in important positions to make changes that can have a positive impact on youth development. However, the very manner in which the system expects these adults to manage student behavior deters them from being adults who form caring, positive relationships with students, especially those students considered at risk within the system. It should not be a surprise if such a student does not view adults as looking out for his or her best interests when those adults enforce rules that the student views as unclear, capricious, unfair, and inconsistently applied.

School communities must challenge youth to believe in and act on the understanding that a nonviolent, pluralistic society is a realistic goal and that there is a need-fulfilling place for them in it. This societal goal will come alive for students only when they can live it in a context significant to their lives. School can be that context. When the adults in that context visualize a peaceable school and commit themselves to actions to achieve constructive conflict resolution in the total school environment, students can embrace that vision and contribute to creating a respectful, compassionate, democratic school and society. When one considers that school is the last remaining collective or common experience for our young people, what other context could this be?

Systems Change

Creating a future generation of responsible, compassionate, caring citizens requires a consistent, comprehensive, sustained effort. That goal will not be realized if students never or only occasionally participate in the workings of a peaceable classroom during their school experience. Although the classroom is the vehicle for promoting emotional intelligence, all classrooms must be united in the effort. The peaceable school is a collective of peaceable classrooms united by a management system that promotes—actually expects—cooperation and eliminates coercive management. But a school is more than a collective of classrooms. Even in a school of self-contained classrooms, students interact with students from other classrooms in the halls, in the restrooms, in the cafeteria, and in other common areas. They also interact across classrooms during the time immediately before and after the formal instructional day. The management plan is for all interactions. When the goals of the peaceable school are realized, the school is a productive place where students and teachers together approach conflicts, including those conflicts labeled misbehavior, as an opportunity for growth. In the process of creating the peaceable school, both educators and students gain life skills that benefit them not just in the school, but also at home, in the community, and in their present and future roles as citizens in a democratic society. For this reason, the program described in *Creating the Peaceable School*[9] is a "high leverage" systems change that results in a learning environment that supports, challenges, and expects intellectual development—emotional and cognitive.

The unifying management system eliminates coercion in favor of cooperation and self-evaluation. The system is the whole school. We contend that this system is a viable vehicle for developing emotionally intelligent youth as well as an effective behavior management program for creating a peaceful climate within the whole school. *Peace* is defined as that state in which every individual is able to survive and thrive without being hampered by conflict, prejudice, hatred, antagonism, or injustice. Peace is not a static state of being, but rather a continual process of interaction based on a philosophy that espouses nonviolence, compassion, trust, fairness, cooperation, respect, and tolerance. It is important to realize that peace is not the absence of conflict. When conflict occurs, as it inevitably will, it is recognized, managed, and resolved in ways that allow each individual to satisfy his or her basic needs while respecting the rights of others. This is no less true because the conflict highlights unfulfilled behavioral expectations.

The classroom is the place where students develop emotional competencies and gain the knowledge base and the foundation abilities needed to resolve conflicts creatively. When the classrooms throughout the school are united by a common vision and an understandable, consistent delivery plan, youth receive a clear message that peace is possible—each can honor himself or herself, honor others, and honor the environment. If this is the credo by which each individual lives in the school, destructive approaches to conflicts diminish in frequency and intensity. Constructive conflict resolution can become "the way we do things here," and destructive approaches will become unacceptable not just to the adult managers but to all members of the school community. These behaviors will be practiced and exhibited, not just in the classroom, but throughout the school.

The classroom teacher is a key player in providing the learning opportunities required to create a peaceable environment in the school as well as in exemplifying the behaviors expected of a peacemaker. However, every adult in the school environment—principal, subject specialist, counselor, social worker, psychologist, secretary, librarian, and so on—is a potential teacher of the concepts and behaviors of peace. All adults in the school are in a position to teach, if not didactically, then by example. Students learn from what they observe: either appropriate and desirable behavior or inappropriate and undesirable behavior. Each person in the school must be cognizant of his or her responsibility in this regard. If we are not modeling what we intend to teach, we are teaching something else. For a school to become a peaceable place, the coercive behaviors of both adults and children must be replaced with the abilities and strategies of conflict resolution. When students are expected and empowered to behave as peacemakers—provided the skills and the opportunity—they will develop and increasingly exhibit emotional intelligence. Coercive behaviors are well entrenched in our society, thus in our schools. These behaviors, especially of the adult managers, will likely not be vanquished through good intentions alone.

Behavior change requires systems modifications to redefine management purpose and practice. More than any other systems feature, the behavior management program and its implementation sets the interactive tone of the classroom and the school. If the goal is to extinguish coercive behavior among students and create a community of caring individuals, it is imperative that we provide programs, strategies, and skills allowing the adults in the system to abandon coercive behavior without abandoning management responsibilities to maintain order. Can we commit to make the required systemic changes and to provide the training and support for staff to learn to function effectively in that reconstituted system?

Endnotes

1. M. J. Elias, J. E. Zins, R. P. Weissberg, K. S. Frey, M. T. Greenberg, N. M. Haynes, R. Kessler, M. E. Schwab-Stone, and T. P. Shriver, *Promoting Social and Emotional Learning: Guidelines for Educators* (Alexandria, VA: Association for Supervision and Curriculum Development, 1997), 1.

2. T. P. Shriver and R. P. Weissberg, "No New Wars!" *Education Week* 15 May (1996), 33, 37.

3. W. J. Kreidler, *Creative Conflict Resolution: More Than 200 Activities for Keeping Peace in the Classroom K–6* (Glenview, IL: Scott, Foresman, 1984), 3.

4. D. W. Johnson and R. T. Johnson, *Reducing School Violence through Conflict Resolution* (Alexandria, VA: Association for Supervision and Curriculum Development, 1995), 14.

5. H. J. Freiberg, "From Tourists to Citizens in the Classroom," *Educational Leadership 54* (1996), 32–36.

6. R. J. Bodine and D. K. Crawford, "Democratizing Schools: Bridging School Behavioral Expectations and Responsible Citizenship in All Life Contexts," *The Fourth R 83* (1998), 5–6.

7. A. Kohn, *Beyond Discipline: From Compliance to Community* (Alexandria, VA: Association for Supervision and Curriculum Development, 1996).

8. Kohn, *Beyond Discipline*, 32.

9. R. J. Bodine, D. K. Crawford, and F. Schrumpf, *Creating the Peaceable School: A Comprehensive Program for Teaching Conflict Resolution* (Champaign, IL: Research Press, 1994).

CHAPTER 4

A Psychological Framework for Managing the Classroom for Emotional Intelligence

Understanding the psychological framework that supports, defines, and provides the foundation for a behavior management system is essential to the achievement of quality performance within that system, whether it is the performance quality of those managed or the performance quality of the managers. No one consistently performs quality work or behaves responsibly when he or she feels threatened or coerced. The same is true when work or behavior is rewarded or punished—this applies to those managed and to those doing the managing. Under such conditions, people tend to do the minimum of what is expected and are not as creative as they otherwise would be.

Accepting that much, if not all, of what is viewed as misbehavior in school is actually conflict for which a constructive resolution has not yet been advanced provides a framework for dealing with unacceptable and nonproductive behaviors. Conflict is a discord of needs, drives, wishes, and/or demands. Three basic categories of conflict exist: Intrapersonal conflict involves an internal discord, interpersonal conflict involves discord between two parties, and intergroup conflict is discord within a group of people or between groups of people. Each of these types of conflict has an impact on schools.

Intrapersonal conflict often goes undetected in social settings and is rarely seen in students as misbehavior until it is manifested as either interpersonal or intergroup conflict. Insight into the true nature of intrapersonal conflict through understanding why one has chosen certain present behaviors and that one has the potential to choose different behaviors may keep intrapersonal conflicts from growing into interpersonal or intergroup ones. Interpersonal and intergroup conflicts are expressed in schools between and among students, between students and adults, and between adults. Student conflicts with adults take at least two forms: One form is an actual interpersonal conflict between the student and the adult; the other, a conflict with the adult because the adult is attempting to gain the student's compliance to system expectations—the conflict is really with the system, but the adult becomes the target. Because of this reality, programs that allow only for conflict resolution between and among students miss the mark. Probably many more conflicts are between students and adults. Since conflicts also exist between adults, and many students are aware of them, not providing for constructive means to deal with those conflicts likely contributes to a distorted view of conflict resolution. Students may think, This is just another thing they expect us to do, but it has no real value in adulthood. Is conflict resolution something we wish children to do but do not expect to apply to adult problems?

To counteract misbehavior within the school it is useful to operationalize the view that conflict is a natural, vital part of life. When conflict is truly understood, it can become an opportunity to learn and create. The synergy of conflict can create new alternatives—something that was not possible before. The challenge, then, is for people in conflict to apply the principles of creative cooperation in their human relationships. When differences are acknowledged and appreciated—and when the conflicting parties build on one another's strengths—a climate is created that nurtures the self-worth of each individual and provides opportunities for fulfillment to each.[1] This approach to conflict is imperative to developing emotionally intelligent individuals. The behavior management system must embrace constructive conflict resolution—building in processes whereby those directly involved with conflict work together for a mutually satisfactory resolution.

According to Kohn, faced with what we perceive to be misbehavior, we operate as if only two responses are possible: punitive action or inaction.[2] Until this false dichotomy (punishing versus doing nothing) is identified and eradicated, we cannot hope to move beyond punitive tactics or rewards designed to control. To move forward, we must understand how and why individuals behave. A program that allows each individual's comprehension of the how and why of his or her behavior to grow continuously is the foundation for developing responsible behavior, and responsible behavior is the hallmark of an emotionally intelligent individual.

Most discipline programs or behavior management methods are based on stimulus-response psychology and focused on extrinsic motivation through rewards and punishments. Much of what takes place in schools emerges from a set of assumptions about human nature based on stimulus-response psychology. These assumptions are inherent not only in the way students are disciplined but also in the view that attempts to control their actions are discipline; not only in the way students are graded but also in the fact that grades are regarded as a way to improve achievement; not only in teachers' orders to students not to interact during work time but also in the fact that student interaction is seen as extraneous to the learning process. These extrinsically motivated management practices—*extrinsic* meaning not part of the essential nature of the individual—rest on the theory that humans can be externally controlled through rewards and punishments.[3]

According to stimulus-response psychology, individuals are controlled by events outside themselves—their behavior is their *response* to external *stimulus*. Under the stimulus-response paradigm, we answer the telephone because it rings and stop the car because the traffic light is red; students stop running down the hall because we tell them to walk. From the stimulus-response perspective, behavior is caused by someone or something (the stimulus) outside the individual: The action following is the response to that stimulus. Following this thinking, to control another one simply controls the stimulus—punish or reward. This is the core belief expressed by most of the discipline systems employed in schools. The only role a manager can assume under such a system is a coercive one. The manager's behavior choice is between hard and soft strategies of coercion (i.e., punishment or reward). In either scenario the goal is to get another to do what you want them to do—to gain their compliance to your expectations.

To further understand the inefficacy of the stimulus-response paradigm, consider the logical viewpoint that this paradigm affords the person exhibiting any behavior with the perfect excuse for behaving in that manner. If it is true that behavior is controlled by external factors, the person is not actually responsible for the behavior; the external stimulus causes the behavior. As Flip Wilson said frequently in a once-popular TV program, "The devil made me do it!" The person exhibiting the behavior is actually a victim of his or her circumstance, of the environment—the behavior is simply a reaction to his or her perceived or actual provocation. For the individual to change his or her behavior, that which is creating the provocation must be altered. In reality, an individual has little actual control over the behavior of others or over the environment. Under such a belief system, a person in the role of behavior manager in actuality becomes responsible for changing someone else's life circumstances, rather than for establishing that the responsibility for behavior is the individual's own. There is no shift to self-responsibility. It is reasonable, consistent with the underlying psychology, to operate as though the individual is only doing what is expected, reacting to external stimuli. Therefore, when the goal is to change behavior, changing the stimulus is required. However, most of the behavior changes attempted in schools are attempted through punishments or rewards focusing on the behavior. A major fallacy in the operation of such a behavior management system is that punishments or rewards are not simply the end result of action. These management plans are built upon the belief that the mere threat of punishment will cause the individual to respond in an appropriate manner; avoiding punishment, then, is really the stimulus. Likewise, reaping the reward becomes the stimulus. The adult managers seem reluctant to ask, What about the environment or the student's condition could we change so the student would respond differently? That strategy would, at least, be consistent with the stimulus-response paradigm. Instead, the adult judges the student's behavior as unacceptable and then expects the student to behave in an acceptable manner. The message is, You do not have to do what you are doing—do something else. Perhaps this is not bad advice. The problem is not that adults—teachers, parents, others—do not know how to tell young people to behave. The problem is that young people too often do not follow adult advice. But then, how well do adults accept unsolicited advice? In fact, adults often invoke the stimulus-response theory to justify their own behavior. Aren't we more willing to excuse our own behavior based on external conditions than we are to accord the same privilege to another whose behavior we find annoying? Almost all of us have blamed a bad mood and subsequent thoughtless behavior on being stressed out by life circumstances—or even on bad weather. But is the same excuse equally acceptable from a young person who has been verbally or physically abusive?

In contrast, a behavior management system designed to help individuals accept responsibility for their behavior requires a psychology that enables the individual to understand the how and why of his or her behavior in terms of factors he or she can choose to control. Key to this notion is an understanding of *intrinsic motivation*. Intrinsic motivation comes from within each individual. It is a part of one's internal system, and it is essential to the nature of the individual. Based on the understanding that people are born with a need for relationships with other people, this view emphasizes that the need for self-esteem, love, and respect are innate. If people are denied dignity and self-esteem (an actual outcome, if not an intended one, of external control systems), intrinsic motivation is suppressed. The management method espoused in this book recognizes the notion that extrinsic motivation is submission to external forces that neutralize intrinsic motivation. This method is committed to management processes that restore power to the individual rather than cause the individual to submit to extrinsic forces. In schools where extrinsic motivation methods are utilized (rewards such as gold stars, happy-face stickers, privileges, adult attention, grades, or the avoidance of punishments), learning and joy of learning in school are suppressed. The student's focus is on working for the grade or the star or the attention, or avoiding the punishment, and consequently the student is divested of the joy and pride that one innately receives from learning itself. Although not its intention, management based on extrinsic motivation may be the major reason so few students are doing quality work or otherwise behaving acceptably in schools.

How and Why People Behave

The operational perspective for the management system embraced here is the psychology of *control theory*. Control theory views motivation as something that causes a given action and that actually comes from within the individual. In other words, each individual's behavior can be driven only by his or her internal system. Therefore, motivation can only be intrinsic, and individuals choose all of their actions. Only the individual has control over those actions, no one else. When managers attempt to control behavior through extrinsic methods, they destroy what they are attempting to create in the first place, a motivated individual.

Understanding internal motivation is critical to becoming an effective manager of behavior facilitative of the development of emotional intelligence. The reality is that to understand effective behavior management, one must understand that *extrinsic motivation* is an oxymoron; *intrinsic motivation,* a redundancy.[4] All motivation is intrinsic.

Control theory explains why (and, to a great extent, how) all living organisms behave. Under this theory, everything we do in life is behavior; all of our behavior is purposeful, and the purpose is always to attempt to satisfy basic needs that are built into our genetic structure. The theory is called control theory because all behavior is our best attempt at the moment to control ourselves (so that we can control the world around us) as we continually try to satisfy one or more of these basic needs. Control theory is based on the assumption that all behavior represents the individual's constant attempt to satisfy one or more of five basic, inborn needs. As William Glasser explains in his exposition of control theory, conflict originates from within.[5] This psychology, therefore, provides not only a general framework for understanding our own and others' behavior, it also offers a workable view of the origins of conflict—what we frequently view as misbehavior in schools.

According to the control theory paradigm, people or events outside us never stimulate us to do anything. Rather, our behavior always represents the choice to do what most satisfies our needs at the time. From this perspective, we follow the rules of a game to achieve a meaningful outcome. We answer the telephone because we choose to do so in order to communicate, not because we react to the ring. We stop at a red light because we choose to avoid risking a traffic ticket or an accident, not because the light has turned red. Likewise, if students stop running down the hall it is because they choose to walk in the belief that walking is more need fulfilling at the moment. When we repeat a choice that is consistently satisfying, we exercise less and less deliberation in making that choice. But even a quick action is chosen, not automatic.

Basic Psychological Needs and Internal Motivation

All individuals are driven by genetically transmitted needs that serve as instructions for attempting to live our lives. The needs are equally important, and all must be reasonably satisfied if individuals are to fulfill their biological destiny. These basic needs are the need to survive, the need to belong, the need to gain power, the need to be free, and the need to have fun. The individual has no choice but to feel pain when a need is frustrated and pleasure when it is satisfied. When any need goes unsatisfied, there is a continual urge to behave. This urge is as much a part of human genetic instructions as is eye color. Instructions related to survival—such as hunger, thirst, and sexual desire—are relatively distinct. Individuals quickly learn that the particular discomfort is attached to this need, and it is plain what they must do to satisfy the survival instructions. The nonsurvival, or psychological, needs are challenging because it is often less clear what an individual must do to satisfy them. Psychological needs, like biological needs, have their source in the genes, even though they are much less tangible and the behaviors that fulfill them are more complex than the physical behaviors used to fulfill the survival needs. Glasser holds that we are essentially biological beings, and the fact that we follow some of our genetic instructions psychologically rather than physically makes neither the instructions less urgent nor the source less biological.

Individuals are all driven by the following four psychological needs:

1. The need to belong—fulfilled by loving, sharing, and cooperating with others
2. The need for power—fulfilled by achieving, accomplishing, and being recognized and respected
3. The need for freedom—fulfilled by making choices in our lives
4. The need for fun—fulfilled by laughing and playing

These needs seem to conflict with one another, and the constant challenge to satisfy them requires continual renegotiation of balance. For example, when a person chooses to work long hours, his accomplishments may help to meet his power need, but he may not be involved with his friends and family in a need-fulfilling way. Perhaps another individual derives a sense of freedom from living alone but loses a sense of belonging when she exercises this choice. Everyone knows a golfer who struggles to balance the need for fun and the need for belonging, met by spending time on weekends with family. When basic needs conflict within an individual, intrapersonal conflict results. Our behavior is what we choose to do to resolve the conflict.

Even though individuals may not be fully aware of their basic needs, they learn that there are some general circumstances that strongly relate to the way they feel. For example, people behave lovingly with their parents because it feels good; they realize that when people pay attention to their words or actions they feel powerful; by making choices they feel the importance of freedom; and through laughter they learn about fun. Degree of awareness aside, an individual has no choice but to feel pain when a basic need is frustrated and pleasure when it is satisfied. When any need goes unsatisfied, there is a continual urge to behave. When that urge generates a behavior that causes difficulty for that individual or, more commonly, when the behavior creates problems for another, the behavior is labeled misbehavior. It is, however, only a behavior and labeling it does not make it otherwise. The individual has chosen a behavior that he or she believes is the best option available to alleviate the pain. When issues surface with others, it is because that behavior choice constitutes a conflict. Most every conflict between people involves attempts to meet one or more of the basic psychological needs of belonging, power, freedom, and fun.

Quality World

Although human needs are essentially the same for everyone, the behaviors through which individuals choose to satisfy those needs may be quite different. Beginning at birth, individuals have unique experiences that feel either pleasurable or painful. Through these experiences, individuals learn how to satisfy their needs. Because individuals have different experiences, the things they learn to do to satisfy their needs will be different as well. Each individual has memories of need-fulfilling behaviors specific to his or her unique life experiences. These pleasurable memories constitute the individual's *quality world* and become the most important part of the person's life. For most people, this quality world is composed of pictures (or, more accurately, perceptions) representing what they have most enjoyed in life. These perceptions become the standard for behavior choices. Unlike the basic survival needs, which are the same for everyone, the perceptions in each person's quality world are very specific and completely individual. Individuals choose to behave in different ways to fulfill their needs because their quality worlds are different. To be in effective control of one's life means integrating this knowledge into the way one deals with others. However, one individual's choice may limit or disrupt another's free choice. This is one significant source of conflict between individuals, especially in social situations like school, where the choice to disassociate from one another is nearly nonexistent. The different choices for need fulfillment of different individuals are the basis for interpersonal and intergroup conflict. In these conflicts our chosen behavior is to do what we believe has the best potential to satisfy our needs. Making choices that protect one's own rights without infringing on the rights of another is a basic precept of conflict resolution and the essence of effective citizenry in a democratic society. This is the working embodiment of responsibility. Each person has no choice but to strive for ultimate need satisfaction; in social settings one must do so without denying the same opportunity to all others. Given the inevitability of conflict, this coupling of responsibility and conflict is the goal of the behavior management program.

Total Behavior

To satisfy the basic needs, a person must behave. This means acting, thinking, feeling, and involving the body, all of which are components of the *total behavior* generated in the effort to get what is wanted. Whenever there is a discrepancy between what one wants and what one has, the internal behavioral system is activated. This is because all humans function as control systems: Their motivation is always to control, not only for present needs but, after those are satisfied, for future needs. People innately reject being controlled by others because they are capable of fulfilling their own needs—indeed, that is the purpose of the control system. Loss of control to another is dysfunctional and runs counter to the fulfillment of needs. This is the root cause of many of the conflicts evidenced in schools between students and adults. It is also the root cause of many of the conflicts between adults. One who perceives a loss of control strives to gain control, always choosing to do so in the manner he or she believes offers the best chance for success.

To satisfy needs, people must be able to sense what is going on both around them and within them, and then be able to act on that information. When we sense a discrepancy between what we have and what we want, we behave by acting upon the world and upon ourselves as a part of the world. All we can do is behave. If we examine this behavior, it may seem to be composed of four different behaviors, but these are actually four components of what is always a total behavior. These four components, which always occur synchronously, are as follows:

1. Doing (e.g., walking, talking)
2. Thinking (e.g., reasoning, fantasizing)
3. Feeling (e.g., angering, depressing)
4. Physiology (e.g., sweating, headaching)

The feeling component of behavior is typically the most obvious to the behaving person. We thus identify the behavior by this predominant component, even though all components are always present and are consistent with one another. The more a person can recognize that feelings are just one component of total behavior, the more the person will be in control of his or her life. The value of recognizing total behavior is that doing so enables a person to control behavior to satisfy his or her needs more effectively. In most situations, a person is more attuned to feelings than to actions, thoughts, or physiology. By recognizing that the feeling component is just one of four that make up total behavior, a person can be more in control of his or her life.

When one begins to think in terms of total behavior, one can see that it is possible to choose these behaviors, as well as to change them. The way to change a total behavior is to change the behavior's doing and thinking components. One has almost total control over the doing component of behavior and some control over the thinking component, less control over the feeling component and almost no control over physiological phenomena. Behavior in its totality ultimately gives one control over all components. When one changes what one is doing, one will notice that thoughts, feelings, and physiological responses change as well. The message is, Because people always have control over the doing component of behavior, if they change that component, they cannot avoid changing the thinking, feeling, and physiological components. To get their needs met effectively, people must realize that they always have control over the doing component and can choose to do something more effective than their present behavior. It may not be easy, but it is always an option. Each individual, in every situation, has a choice to behave differently. One can always choose a new behavior—actually, a new total behavior. An effective behavior management system assists individuals to evaluate their present behavior and generate other behavioral options. This is done in the meaningful context of satisfying basic psychological needs by focusing attention on and planning for the doing component, that component over which the individual has the most control. The management challenge is to assist or cause the individual to focus on this component rather than the component of which the individual is most aware—feeling. If behavior change could be affected by focusing on feelings, wouldn't most of us tell ourselves frequently to "just feel better"?

Thus, even though all people are driven by the same four needs, each person's wants—or pictures—are unique. It is impossible for two people to have the same picture album (quality world) because it is impossible for two people to live exactly the same life. These differences are the essence of conflict. If a person wishes to understand conflict and perceive it positively, the knowledge that no two people can have exactly the same wants is central. For example, if two individuals wish to satisfy their need to belong through a friendship, they must learn to share their commonalities and respect and value their differences.

As long as people have conflicting wants and as long as an individual's needs can be satisfied in ways that may conflict, the need to renegotiate balance will persist. Thus, driven by our genetic instructions, we will inevitably experience conflict. When individuals conflict, they have only two choices—to continue to conflict or to problem solve. If they choose to continue to conflict, their behavior choice is coercion—attempt to get the other person to do what you want. Given this reality, it is reasonable to assume that a behavior management program could be devised to assist individuals to understand their own behavior, the behavior of others, and the relationship between the two. This type of understanding is a basic necessity for problem solving. What role would managers assume under such a program? Isn't it obvious that they should not model coercion if they wish to encourage others to avoid coercion and choose to problem solve instead?

Reality Therapy

Reality therapy is a method of counseling, developed by William Glasser, based on control theory and aimed at helping individuals to gain more effective control over their own lives.[6] Individuals can also use it to improve their own effectiveness—the ultimate goal. This process has been proven effective in education, parenting, leadership, and management: It lends itself to any situation where people need to learn how to satisfy their needs in responsible ways. Reality therapy is based on the belief that we all choose what we do with our lives and that we are responsible for the choices. *Responsibility* is defined as learning to choose behaviors that satisfy our needs and, at the same time, do not deprive others of a chance to do the same. Practitioners of reality therapy persuade individuals to look honestly at both what they want and what they are doing to get what they want. An individual who is frustrated, or is frustrating others, is taught to evaluate what he or she is doing and, from this evaluation, learns about and puts into practice more effective (need-satisfying) behaviors.[7] Reality therapy is a method that is effective in interpersonal and intergroup conflict in addition to being effective in helping the individual in need of therapy to handle his or her intrapersonal conflicts constructively.

Educators can use reality therapy with students in the classroom and school as a process to facilitate the evaluation of student work, to plan group and individualized learning experiences, and to manage behavior. Reality therapy is a flowing and adaptable communication process that allows educators to create a supportive environment within which individuals are free to do quality learning and exhibit quality behavior.

Reality therapy helps people learn to be in effective control of their lives. It is a noncoercive method of communicating with people that enhances people's ability to make effective, need-fulfilling choices. Reality therapy is an ongoing process with two major components: (a) the counseling environment and (b) specific procedures that lead to changes in behavior. The art of reality therapy is to join these components in ways that lead people to evaluate their lives and decide to move in more effective directions.

Counseling Environment

Reality therapy requires a supportive environment within which individuals can begin to make changes in their lives. Following are tiered guidelines, each dependent upon and building upon the ones preceding, for creating this personalized environment:

1. Be friendly and listen to the person.

2. Do not allow the person to focus on past events unless those events relate immediately to the present situation.

3. Avoid discussing feelings or physiology responses as though they were separate from total behaviors; always relate feelings and physiology to concurrent actions and thoughts over which the person has more direct control.

4. Accept no excuses for irresponsible behavior, particularly when a person fails to do what he or she has expressed an intention to do.

5. Avoid punishing, criticizing, or attempting to protect the person from the reasonable consequences of his or her chosen behavior.

Crucial to the counseling environment is involvement characterized by mutual trust and caring. In the absence of involvement, people will not be willing to risk making changes in their lives. A manager who chooses to manage through coercion will not generate the required level of involvement to assist another to engage in self-sustainable behavior change.

Procedures That Lead to Change

To encourage change through reality therapy, the manager has specific procedures to follow—not necessarily always in the order presented here, but rather entwined in a holistic manner appropriate to the person and the circumstance.

1. Focus on the person's total behavior—the way he or she is acting, thinking, and feeling now. Help the person to learn the difficult lesson that all total behavior is chosen, however painful and self-destructive it may be.

2. Ask the person what he or she wants now—look at the present pictures of the quality world. Then expand the questioning into the directions he or she would like to take in life. If the answer is "I don't know," continue to focus on what the person is doing now (total behavior) to reinforce the understanding that the present direction is the result of choice.

3. Ask the person to make the following evaluation: "Does your present behavior have a reasonable chance of getting you what you want now, and will it take you in the direction you want to go?"

4. If the answer is no (meaning that desired direction is reasonable but the present behavior will not take the person there), help the person plan new behavior.

5. If the answer is no but the person seems unable to get what he or she wants no matter how much effort is made, ask questions that facilitate changing directions. In this case, the focus becomes more on changing what the person wants than on the behavior itself.

6. If the answer is yes (meaning the person sees nothing wrong with the present behavior or desired direction), continue to focus on the present behaviors and keep repeating the evaluative question (number 3 above) in a variety of ways. Move toward the questions "How is your behavior affecting others?" and "Is your behavior helping anyone else?"

7. Obtain an agreement upon a plan that has a good chance to succeed and ask the person for a commitment to follow through with it. A written plan may generally be more effective in sealing a commitment.

8. Do not give up on the person's ability to achieve a more responsible life, even if the person makes little effort to follow through on the plans. Giving up tends to confirm the person's belief that no one cares enough to help.

In following the procedures for change, it is important to keep in mind that people choose their total behavior even though one or more of the individual components may not be chosen. Also, remember as well that, however ineffective or self-destructive a behavior may appear, it is always the best that the person believes he or she can do. In that sense, the behavior is "effective" for the individual. This is precisely why change is difficult. A person will not make a change in behavior until the following two prerequisites are met: (a) using his or her own evaluation, an individual must decide that present behavior will either not attain what is desired or take the person in the desired direction and (b) an individual must believe that he or she has available another behavior that will permit his or her needs to be satisfied reasonably well.

Reality therapy teaches that people can live their lives most successfully when they acknowledge and accept accountability for their chosen behaviors. The practitioner of reality therapy, for our purposes in this book the behavior manager, should never doubt that people are able to choose more responsible and effective behaviors. It is up to the practitioner to help the individual avoid excuses and accept this responsibility, and to provide opportunities for the individual to learn and test new and more effective behavioral choices. Because we operate in a social context, eventually the behavior must meet both the condition of improved need satisfaction to the individual and contribute to, or at least not detract from, the sense of community. The concept of total behavior, the individual's knowing that he or she can always choose to do something different, backs up the behavior manager's expectation that a logical consequence for a socially unacceptable behavior is the requirement to choose a different action.

Endnotes

1. R. J. Bodine, D. K. Crawford, and F. Schrumpf, *Creating the Peaceable School: A Comprehensive Program for Teaching Conflict Resolution* (Champaign, IL: Research Press, 1994).

2. A. Kohn, *Beyond Discipline: From Compliance to Community* (Alexandria, VA: Association for Supervision and Curriculum Development, 1996).

3. D. K. Crawford, R. J. Bodine, and R. G. Hoglund, *The School for Quality Learning: Managing the School and Classroom the Deming Way* (Champaign, IL: Research Press, 1993).

4. Crawford et al., *The School for Quality Learning.*

5. W. Glasser, *Control Theory: A New Explanation of How We Control Our Lives* (New York: Harper and Row, 1984).

6. Glasser, *Control Theory.*

7. Crawford et al., *The School for Quality Learning.*

CHAPTER 5

A Management System for Creating Responsible Learners and Citizens

Kohn observes, "To help students become ethical people, as opposed to people who merely do what they are told, we cannot merely tell them what to do. We have to help them figure out—for themselves and with each other—how one ought to act. That's why dropping the tools of traditional discipline, like rewards and punishments, is only the beginning. It's even more crucial that we overcome a preoccupation with getting compliance and instead involve students in devising and justifying ethical principles."[1]

A Process, Not a Recipe

It seems clear that the development of emotional intelligence to create responsible learners in our schools and ultimately to develop responsible citizens for our world is a process, not a recipe. What then is the relationship between behavior management and emotional intelligence? Knowing the relationship, how can a management program be constructed to take advantage of that relationship and develop emotionally intelligent individuals? A successful management program has two dimensions: (a) an instructional component that provides the knowledge base for understanding individual behavior and for understanding behavioral expectations of the system and (b) strategies for managing behavior within the system, which provides a learning laboratory for choosing appropriate, need-fulfilling behaviors and for the transfer of those learnings to other life contexts.

A behavior management program would facilitate development in all five domains of emotional ability identified by Salovey and Mayer in their definition of emotional intelligence: (a) knowing one's emotions, (b) managing emotions, (c) motivating oneself, (d) recognizing emotions in others, and (e) handling relationships.[2] The cornerstone of the behavior management program delineated in this book is creating self-awareness through questioning strategies utilized by the manager to assist or cause the learner to focus attention on his or her own total behavior. Learning to know one's emotions and learning to manage them are the basic entry points to the development of emotional intelligence. The manager who wishes to promote emotional intelligence and to develop socially workable behaviors from those managed attempts to advance self-awareness in these critical dimensions.

Teachable Behaviors and Facilitative Probes

We know that feelings are only one component of a total behavior—but often the one the individual is most aware of initially. A successful program will build in learning opportunities to extend an understanding of emotions beyond the limited "mad-sad-glad" repertoire of many students. Helping students learn to recognize and communicate about emotions at a more sophisticated level legitimizes emotions within the learning environment. Family groupings of feeling words such as the following are useful in teaching:

- Anger: Fury, outrage, resentment, wrath, exasperation, indignation, vexation, acrimony, animosity, annoyance, irritability, hostility

- Sadness: Grief, sorrow, cheerlessness, gloom, melancholy, self-pity, loneliness, dejection, despair

- Fear: Anxiety, apprehension, nervousness, concern, consternation, misgiving, wariness, qualm, edginess, dread, fright, terror, panic

- Enjoyment: Happiness, joy, relief, contentment, bliss, delight, amusement, pride, sensual pleasure, thrill, rapture, gratification, satisfaction, euphoria, whimsy, ecstasy

- Love: Acceptance, friendliness, trust, kindness, affinity, devotion, adoration, infatuation
- Surprise: Shock, astonishment, amazement, wonder, agape
- Disgust: Contempt, disdain, scorn, abhorrence, aversion, distaste, revulsion
- Shame: Guilt, embarrassment, chagrin, remorse, humiliation, regret, mortification, contrition[3]

This family categorization of emotions may not be scientifically defensible, but it shows the broad range of descriptors available for communicating the emotional content of behavior. In addition, there are classic blends such as jealousy (a variant of anger that melds sadness and fear) and virtue (hope and faith, courage and forgiveness, certainty and equanimity). Also, there are classic vices, feelings such as doubt, complacency, sloth, or boredom.[4]

It is a teachable ability to extend vocabulary to increase one's options for talking about the emotional content of behavior. Facilitative probes to encourage expanded emotional expression are "Can you use words to tell how you are feeling?" and "Can you be any more precise?"

A *teachable ability* is an ability that can be developed in individuals through the process of facilitative learning. Teachable abilities encompass attitudes, understandings, and skills that are, when mastered, translated into behavior. A *facilitative probe* is a question, directive, or suggestion by a behavior manager (teacher, parent, etc.) that prompts another to evaluate his or her own behavior. The facilitative probe focuses the learner's attention on his or her developing ability to choose new behaviors. When a teachable ability has been developed and when a management system as advocated here is in place, such probes can become a primary management tool.

Assisting students to grow in self-awareness, a necessary condition for emotional intelligence, involves facilitating learning opportunities to help them accomplish the following:

1. Examine how they make judgments and assessments.
2. Tune in to the sensory data available to them.
3. Get in touch with their feelings.
4. Gain awareness of their intentions.
5. Attend to their actions.[5]

Our judgments and assessments are all the different impressions, interpretations, evaluations, and expectations we have about ourselves, other people, and situations. These are influenced by unique individual factors that shape our personality, such as family background, previous experience, natural abilities, prior learning, and systems of belief. Our judgments and assessments generally take the form of thoughts. The emotionally intelligent individual understands that these thoughts may be, and most often are, more about perceived reality than actual reality. He or she recognizes that it is these judgments, not someone else's behavior or an event, that drives his or her behavior. It is the personal meaning that we assign to events and to people that affects us positively or negatively, not the events or the people themselves. The emotionally intelligent recognize that thoughts or judgments are not immutable; they are subject to change based on new information that self-awareness processes can provide.

A teachable ability is learning to engage in an inner dialogue using "I think" statements. Using "I think" statements helps to clarify what one thinks and forces one to recognize that one is responsible for the judgment or assessment. For example, "I think the teacher is unfair because I think he demands more of me than he does of some others" holds a very different meaning than "The teacher is unfair and picks on me." Facilitative probes are, "Can you describe your thoughts at this moment?" "Can you recall what you were thinking when that happened?"

Another teachable ability is to learn to reflect on events or encounters when you are calm. We often make our judgments when we are agitated, and thus our conclusions are more likely to be inaccurate. That is complicated by the human tendency to formulate plans quickly based on our judgments. The emotionally intelligent individual learns not to overcommit to the plan, evaluating the merits of the plan when under less stressful conditions and making appropriate revisions to the plan before taking action. Emotionally intelligent persons also "check out" the validity of their judgments and assessments with others who also were involved in the encounter or event. Others' perspectives provide us important information for deciding whether our view is on target, off base, or somewhere in between. The facilitative probes might be "Would you choose that behavior if you thought carefully about it?" and "If you were calm, what would you choose to do?"

Our senses (seeing, hearing, smelling, tasting, and touching) are the sources of all our data about the world—about ourselves, about other people, and about situations. The emotionally intelligent individual understands that, although our senses collect data from the real world, our personal filters determine what data are perceived and recorded. Further, because of our filters, we interpret the data uniquely. One of the most powerful filters through which our encounters and events are screened is our "snap judgment" about the encounter or event. A teachable ability is to distinguish between sensory data and our judgments or assessments. "You are angry" is different from "I see you have a red face and clenched fists." One might receive the same sensory input from someone in pain. "I think you're excited" is different from "I hear you talking fast and see that you are very animated while talking." A frightened person might also exhibit these behaviors. The higher one's self-awareness, the greater one's ability to take the filtering process into account and to differentiate between sensory data and interpretations of those data. The facilitative probes are "Have you considered all your information?" and "Are there other possible interpretations you could make?"

Feelings are our spontaneous emotional responses to our interpretations and expectations. They can provide important information about why we do what we do. Feelings inform us as to our comfort level in a situation and can help us understand our reactions. However, tuning into our emotions is not something that comes easily to most individuals. To tune into feelings—especially distressing ones such as anger, sadness, and resentment—we must experience them and raise them to the conscious level, and that can be painful. So instead we ignore them, deny them, or rationalize them. This may allow us to avoid feeling bad at the moment, but it also prevents us from making use of the valuable information these feelings could give us and from using our emotions intelligently. By ignoring or denying emotions we deny ourselves the ability to work through them. Negative feelings can often fester, leaving us feeling worse than we would by tuning into them. By acknowledging them, we are able to manage them and move forward.

A teachable ability is learning to pay attention to the physical manifestations associated with our feelings. Although our feelings are internal, certain body signals are usually associated with certain feelings. Anger signals may be hairs standing up on the neck, face suddenly feeling hot, clenched teeth, trembling, or general body tension; embarrassment might be signaled by a general warming of the face; nervousness or anxiety might be signaled by stirrings in the stomach, sweaty palms, or a dry mouth. Also, feelings drive certain behaviors. By examining behavioral manifestations, we can often learn the underlying feeling. Clenching some object in your possession or presence may signal anger; tapping behavior may be a sign of anxiety; spontaneous smiling signals happiness. Although physiological signals and behavioral responses may differ to some extent from individual to individual, each individual can learn to interpret his or her unique manifestations. Anger cues, the physical signs of anger, are often the first manifestations we learn to interpret. Managing anger constructively is one of the earliest social graces most individuals develop. Anger, however, is only one emotion or emotional family, and many other emotions also afford cues we can learn to interpret. The facilitative probes are "Are you tuned into what your body is telling you?" "What are you feeling now?" and "How did you feel when that happened?"

Intentions refer to our immediate desires. Becoming fully aware of our intentions allows us to better strategize a course of action and to achieve what we want. Intentions, like feelings, can be difficult to discern, largely because we confuse one intention with another. We may be aware of our apparent intention but not our hidden agenda. This is akin to what we want versus what we really want or, in the conflict resolution vernacular, *positions* versus *interests*. For example, a student may intend to practice hard at improving her shooting so that she can make the basketball team.

But her hidden agenda might be that she wants her friends, who told her that she was not good enough to be a basketball player, to be impressed. In this case, recognizing her true intentions might not change her plan of action. But membership on the basketball team is likely a more long-term venture than impressing friends and may well require more than bargained for. Also, intentions sometimes conflict. A boy wants to yell at his sister because she failed to give him an important phone message from his girlfriend. But he also wants to maintain a good relationship because she is his sister and because she is his girlfriend's best friend. If he determines that his true intention is to have a good relationship with his sister, he will work to control his anger.

Another teachable ability is to learn to recognize behavior on the basis of choices one makes to satisfy the basic psychological needs of belonging, power, freedom, and fun. These psychological needs underlie our intentions. The facilitative probes are "What behavior are you choosing and why are you choosing that particular behavior?" "What do you really want?" and "What might happen if you do that?" (See the appendix for sample lessons to instill in young people an understanding of basic needs and behavioral choices relative to those needs.)

Our actions are the observable manifestations of our choices to behave and are the culminating events that incorporate our judgments, our sensory input, our feelings, and our intentions. Actions are the component of our total behavior observable to others. But our actions are not always as they seem to us. We are generally aware of our broad actions but are often unaware of the nuances of those actions. It is the nuances—speech patterns, tone of voice, body language, nonverbal behavior—that are frequently apparent to others and that play a large part in how they see us and interpret our behavior. Self-awareness of behavior seems largely to correlate positively with the degree to which the behavior is need fulfilling and socially accepted. Individuals who exhibit behaviors generally judged as negative are likely to be less aware of their behaviors than individuals who exhibit behaviors generally judged as positive. The "failure identity" individual is usually lacking in self-awareness while, at the same time, nearly everyone else associated with that person is very aware of his or her behavior.

A teachable ability is to learn the concept of total behavior and develop an understanding of the degree to which one has control over the components of the total behavior: acting, thinking, feeling, and physiology. Take, for example, a common misbehavior in school, a student angrily talking back to the teacher. The teacher's view may be that this is a pretty uncomplicated behavior—this is just another lazy kid "shooting off his mouth" instead of doing his work. The student probably thinks it's pretty simple also. The teacher got him so upset that he told the teacher off. It's not the student's fault; the teacher deserved it. Here anger is the most obvious component of the student's total behavior, but obvious or not, it is only one of the four components of the total behavior. Most of the angry student's total behavior is conscious and purposeful—like yelling, threatening, and plotting revenge, but some—like getting red in the face, sweating, or trembling with rage—is unconscious and automatic. The point is that, whether conscious or unconscious, it is behavior. For all practical purposes, while one may not choose every part, one almost always chooses the total behavior, which is the sum of all the parts. Usually we have no difficulty accepting that a total behavior is chosen if it is mostly the action and thinking that commands our attention. If the student had calmly slammed his books on the floor or quietly cursed the teacher, he would have little success convincing anyone that he did not choose what he did. But the student doesn't slam and curse calmly and quietly; he behaves with overt anger. He then tries to avoid responsibility by claiming that he was so upset by the teacher that he couldn't help what he did. The student is actually claiming that his feelings, not he, are responsible for what he did, and since his feelings were caused by the teacher, the teacher, not he, is really responsible for the whole outburst.[6]

Remember that our total behavior is chosen and whatever total behavior we choose is always our best attempt to gain effective control of our lives, which means reducing the difference between what we want at the time and what we see is available in the real world.[7] Another teachable ability is to learn to examine how our judgments are affected by the nuances of another's behavior and to self-monitor nuances of our own behavior. The facilitative probes are "What are you doing?"

"What did you do that may have caused the other person to react as he or she did?" "What about the other person's actions caused you to react as you did?" "If you were the other person, what might you think about this situation?" "What might you be feeling?" and "What might you do?"

Managing emotions involves developing an understanding of the emotional mind, which is very different from the rational mind. Effective management strategies allow for the abandonment of the oft-used excuse, "One cannot deal rationally with an irrational (emotional) individual." Some differences between the emotional mind and the rational mind that are likely important in social contexts such as school are as follows:

- The emotional mind is far quicker than the rational mind, springing into action without pausing even a moment to consider what it is doing; we often register awareness of our reaction only after we have already acted.

- Actions that spring from the emotional mind carry a particularly strong sense of certainty and urgency, a by-product of a streamlined, simplified way of looking at things that can absolutely bewilder the rational mind—the "first impulse" in an emotional situation is the heart's, not the head's.

- There is also a second, slower kind of emotional response that flows from thoughts and triggers emotions that are more deliberate, such as embarrassment or apprehension.

- The logic of the emotional mind is associative; that is, it takes elements that symbolize a reality, or trigger a memory of a reality, to be the same as that reality; thus things need not be defined by their objective identity, what matters is how they are perceived—things are as they seem.

- The emotional mind reacts to the present as though it were the past; when some feature of an event seems similar to an emotionally charged past memory, the emotional mind responds by triggering the feelings that went with the remembered event—emotions often occur out-of-time.

- The emotional mind is to a large degree state-specific; that is, each feeling has its own distinct repertoire of thought, reactions, and memories, and these repertoires become predominant in moments of intense emotions.[8]

Managing emotions is actually the diligent effort of inducing the rational mind to regulate the emotional mind.

A teachable ability is the employment of William J. Kreidler's *conflict escalator*.[9] Think of a department store, and visualize the stairsteps of the up escalator. Kreidler maintains that all conflicts escalate, get worse, in a step-by-step manner. However, to many, conflict feels more like an express elevator—one moment you are calm; the next, raging mad. Every action in the conflict is either a step up or a step down the escalator, and any action that makes the conflict worse takes the conflict another step up the escalator. Every step up the conflict escalator has feelings that accompany the action. As the conflict escalates, so does the intensity of the feelings. The higher one goes on the escalator, the harder it is to come down. The conflict escalator is a tool that helps one think about how conflicts begin and what contributes to their escalation. Learning to identify the action and the accompanying feelings of each step better enables one to recognize the elevation and to employ deescalating actions before the conflict reaches the destructive stage—the top of the escalator. Managing emotions involves awareness of feelings and associated actions, then choosing a different action that allows movement down the escalator. The facilitative probes are "Are you choosing to go up the escalator?" "Can you choose differently?" and "What do you need to do to get off the escalator?"

Essential System Contexts

Constructing a behavior management program to promote the development of emotional intelligence requires adoption of the idea that when misbehavior occurs, a proactive rather than reactive response is needed. Toward that end, we approach what is usually viewed as misbehavior as unresolved conflict. This approach provides processes for individuals to recognize and manage emotions intelligently and constructively. Particularly, it addresses planning for behavioral change to create successful relationships through exploring the perceived realities of the conflicting parties. Chapter 7 offers a detailed look at conflict resolution education and explores its viability in extending emotional intelligence to the realm of relationships. The processes of conflict resolution are strategies for planning for different behavior. These processes are dependent upon the acquisition of certain foundation abilities, perhaps the most significant being emotional abilities. Emotional abilities are most significant because the use of the other foundation abilities of conflict resolution require emotional awareness and control. Constructive participation in a conflict resolution process is nearly always dependent upon successful management of emotions. However, having the capability to manage emotions successfully does not necessarily mean one can constructively resolve conflicts. The foundation abilities and the processes of conflict resolution work in concert, but one without the other is unlikely to allow the individual to participate fully in the design of his or her own responsible behavior.

Creating the classroom and school as a laboratory for learning and practicing behaviors of responsible citizenship mandates the establishment of two essential structural and behavioral contexts.

Building Community: A Cooperative Context

One context involves a shift from a largely competitive culture to one characterized by cooperation. Developing a cooperative context within the classroom and school is essential. Emotional intelligence is not developed in isolation, but in interactive circumstances. Responsible citizenship does not occur in a vacuum, but rather in a community. A sense of community, sharing commonalties and caring for others, is an overriding environmental prerequisite if individuals in the community are to learn to live in civil association with others. Conflict resolution that yields responsible, need-fulfilling action plans requires that the conflicting parties cooperate in the problem-solving endeavors. If that is the only time cooperation is expected, conflict resolution processes will likely be seen as aberrant behavior, especially by those who normally do well in competitive pursuits.

In the classroom, as with any collection of individuals, there are two possible responses to conflict—cooperative and competitive. In the competitive context, rewards are restricted to the few who perform the best. Competitors usually have a short-term time orientation and focus all energies on winning. Little, if any, attention is paid to the longer term interest of maintaining good relationships. Competitors typically avoid truly communicating with each other—verbal exchanges are most likely characterized by posturing or are purposely deceitful. Competitors are likely to misperceive the positions and motivations of the others involved, are suspicious of others, and deny the legitimacy of the needs and feelings of others in favor of their own interests. A competitive context creates a Win-Lose approach to resolving conflict.

In contrast, a cooperative context involves goals that all are committed to achieving. Outcomes beneficial to everyone involved are sought. Cooperators typically have a long-term orientation and focus energies both on achieving goals and on maintaining good relationships with others. Cooperators tend to perceive the positions and motivations of others accurately, communicate accurately and thoroughly, hold a positive and trusting attitude toward others, and see conflicts as mutual problems for which solutions can be found.[10]

Johnson and Johnson proclaim that "it makes little sense to teach students to manage conflicts constructively if the school is structured so that students have to compete for scarce rewards (like grades of 'A') and defeat each other to get what they want."[11] The nature of the reward system is an extremely important dimension of the classroom context because it affects both the establishment of the cooperative classroom context and the management of student behavior without coercion.

The primary reward system of nearly every classroom is grades—primary in importance to the recipient, that is. The practice of awarding grades is the ultimate coercive practice. Grades exemplify a competitive context. Defenders of the grading system often argue that competition is fundamental to our society and that participating in a competitive system early on prepares the learner for the realities of life. This argument is based on several myths about competition: that competition is part of human nature and is an inevitable fact of life, that competition motivates one to do one's best, that without competition one would cease to be productive, and that competition in the form of contests is the best way to have fun. Competition in the learning environment, as in any endeavor, creates winners and losers. It also suppresses learners' inclination to work cooperatively. On the other hand, when learners are encouraged to cooperate, combining their talents and energies so that as many as possible can achieve the desired result, the system becomes a Win-Win system. Learning by all individuals is the outcome of a Win-Win system; in the Win-Lose system, grades or adult attention, not learning, are the outcome pursued.[12]

Johnson and Johnson also advance that a cooperative context is best established by structuring most learning situations cooperatively.[13] The teacher who desires to develop emotional intelligence in the classroom implements cooperative learning activities that require collaboration and promote interdependence among class members. The teacher fosters a community-of-learners atmosphere that evokes the feeling that "we are all in this together" and requires learners to help one another actively. Collaboration is the rule; competition is minimized or even temporarily suspended entirely to add emphasis to the goal of collaboration. All learners strive to be the best they can be and to do the best they can do.

The teacher builds a collaborative atmosphere by promoting the following simple notions among the students:

1. If one learner in the group can do something, everyone can learn to do it.

2. Learners working together can accomplish greater results than learners working independently.

3. If you can do something another cannot, you can help that other person reach the same level of success if you provide encouragement and assistance, and exercise patience.

4. In any group (two or more individuals) situation—be the problem mental, physical, or social—"we" are smarter and more creative than "me."[14]

Establishing a cooperative context does not mean eliminating competition; it means striking a balance between competition and cooperation. It means to make clear that cooperation is a desirable behavior in a large variety of endeavors, not just in interpersonal conflicts.

Managing Behavior without Coercion

The other context important in fostering responsible citizenship involves the management of student behavior without coercion. This notion requires that each adult in the school view acceptable behavior as the responsibility of each student and that each student learn to accept this responsibility. The realization of this ideal depends, at least in part, upon the development of knowledge about responsibility—what is it and what choices constitute responsible behavior. The behavior management plan must be noncoercive and incorporate management behaviors that will help the learner acquire the knowledge base necessary for the plan to operate successfully—that is, by choosing responsible behaviors rather than complying to external pressures.

Responsible behavior—the hallmark of an emotionally intelligent individual—depends above all else on the absence of coercion. To coerce is to compel or force another to act or think in a given manner—to dominate, restrain, or control another through the use of actual or implied force. Either overt or covert coercion is the behavioral choice of the individual who views conflict as a contest or a competition. This viewpoint encompasses the idea that "I have to get what I want," likely at someone else's expense, or "I have to make another do what I want." The teacher in the emotionally intelligent classroom abandons as counterproductive the inclination to exercise forceful authority over the learners. Doing so is bad behavior modeling and has no long-term benefit. Forceful authority is counterproductive to the cooperative context, to constructive conflict resolution, and to the acceptance of self-responsibility. The teacher who manages behavior for the development of emotional intelligence transfers the responsibility for acceptable behavior to the students, not through force or domination but through reason and support. In the classroom, the pervasive values touching the interactions between students, between students and adults, and between adults are human dignity and self-esteem.

Noncoercive management practices work because they create a need-fulfilling work environment. In a need-fulfilling school work environment, the students' natural inclination to learn and be creative is nurtured and preserved. Noncoercive management realizes that true motivation is intrinsic and that joy and pride in work is the result. When learners are motivated, quality becomes their goal.

Table 5.1 contrasts total behavior of students under noncoercive management and under the more traditional coercive management style that relies largely on punishment and rewards. Is a student who is complaining, avoiding, fearing, headaching, or daydreaming likely to do quality work, to act responsibly?

When the environment is need fulfilling, the choices available to meet learners' basic needs create opportunities to develop a number of effective, need-fulfilling behaviors that are a part of their quality worlds. Coercive management, by contrast, offers

Table 5.1

Total Behavior of Learners under Different Management Styles

	Learners' behavior	
	Under noncoercive management	**Under coercive management**
Doing	cooperating accomplishing contributing delivering	withdrawing complaining avoiding punishing
Thinking	wondering evaluating	daydreaming judging
Feeling	priding trusting	fearing depressing
Physiology	energizing normal heartbeating	tiring headaching

learners few opportunities to build a repertoire of need-fulfilling behaviors. In fact, traditional coercive management often perpetuates the use of ineffective, unfulfilling behaviors. When learners are managed coercively, work is rarely a part of their quality world. The work environment under coercive management as shown in Table 5.2 provides less opportunity for the satisfaction of our basic psychological needs. Are these individuals likely to develop emotional intelligence?

Considering the psychological effects, coercive management deprives the individual of innate motivation, self-esteem, and dignity while cultivating fear and defensiveness. The result is loss of motivation—more accurately, the diminishing of the capacity to self-motivate, to do quality work.

Punishment or discipline

Are the idea of a discipline program and the notion of behavior management without coercion contradictory? The answer is a resounding no, but the question is understandable. Many existing discipline programs are misnamed. It would be more accurate to call them punishment programs. Punishment is coercive; discipline is educational. Table 5.3 contrasts punishment and discipline.

Punishment is a poor deterrent to undesirable behavior. It often results in an angry recipient, who focuses on revenge behaviors, or a compliant one, who attempts to follow the rules out of fear. Because punishment does not teach appropriate behaviors, it frequently leads to repetition of the undesirable (punished) behavior or the exhibition of an equally undesirable behavior.

Compliance is a recourse for the learner who wishes to avoid punishment. The learner acquiesces to an authority. Behavior change, if any, is usually predicated on fear—either fear of the person in authority or fear of the consequences of not doing as expected. Perhaps one of the main reasons that many school discipline programs no longer work with many students is that those students have no fear—they have already experienced things far worse than the school can or would do to them.

A tendency to yield to others runs counter to the notion of emotional intelligence. Compliance negates thinking: The learner

Table 5.2

Choices for Learners under Different Management Styles

	Basic needs	
	Learner's choices under noncoercive management	Learner's choices under coercive management
Belonging	To share and cooperate with others	To work alone and compete with others
	To contribute to welfare of community—school/classroom	To work for welfare of self
	To see goodness in self and others	To isolate self and mistrust others
Power	To make action plans to achieve	To anger, criticize, and punish to control others
	To take risks and learn new skills	To play it safe
	To think Win-Win	To think Win-Lose
	To be into process as well as into outcome	To be into outcome more than process
Freedom	To brainstorm alternatives to problems	To blame others for problems
	To take action	To make excuses
	To create opportunities	To complain about limits
Fun	To view work as pleasurable	To view work as boring
	To initiate fun activities	To find no time or energy for fun

accepts, at least temporarily, the logic of the authority. The compliant learner does not examine alternative behaviors to find the one that would be most need fulfilling in the given situation. Compliant behavior is also contrary to conflict resolution. Because compliance rarely fulfills one's needs, the compliant behavior tends

Table 5.3
Punishment versus Discipline

Punishment	Discipline
1. Expresses power of an authority; usually causes pain to the recipient; is based upon retribution or revenge; is concerned with what has happened (the past)	1. Is based on logical or natural consequences that embody the reality of a social order (rules that one must learn and accept to function adequately and productively in society); concerned with what is
2. Is arbitrary—probably applied inconsistently and unconditionally; does not accept or acknowledge exceptions or mitigating circumstances	2. Is consistent—accepts that the behaving individual is doing the best he or she can do for now
3. Is imposed by an authority (done to someone), with responsibility assumed by the one administering the punishment and the behaving individual avoiding responsibility	3. Comes from within, with responsibility assumed by the behaving individual and the behaving individual's desiring responsibility; presumes that conscience is internal
4. Closes options for the individual, who must pay for a behavior that has already occurred	4. Opens options for the individual, who can choose a new behavior
5. As a teaching process, usually reinforces a failure identity; essentially negative and short term, without sustained personal involvement of either teacher or learner	5. As a teaching process, is active and involves close, sustained, personal involvement of both teacher and learner; emphasizes developing ways to act that will result in more successful behavior
6. Is characterized by open or concealed anger; is a poor model of the expectations of quality	6. Is friendly and supportive; provides a model of quality behavior
7. Is easy and expedient	7. Is difficult and time consuming
8. Focuses on strategies intended to control behavior of the learner	8. Focuses on the learner's behavior and the consequences of that behavior

9. Rarely results in positive changes in behavior; may increase subversiveness or result in temporary suppression of behavior; at best, produces compliance	9. Usually results in a change in behavior that is more successful, acceptable, and responsible; develops the capacity for self-evaluation of behavior

to be inconsistently displayed in the presence of the authority and often disappears in the absence of the authority. In a classroom setting, it is true that a group of compliant learners are easily managed by the teacher. But the teacher who strives to prepare learners to be responsible citizens in our world understands that quality learning and quality behavior bear little relationship to being compliant. Do we seek persons who follow rules out of fear or through blind obedience, or do we seek persons who follow rules because the rules allow for personal need fulfillment and for civil association?

Punishment frustrates all of the recipient's basic psychological needs (belonging, power, freedom, and fun). The relationship between the recipient and the person administering the punishment is diminished, stymieing the recipient's ability to meet the need for belonging. Because of the negative focus of punishment, the recipient is likely to be ostracized by appropriately behaving peers and may seek out inappropriately behaving peers in an effort to belong. Punishment obviously restricts freedom and is not pleasurable—it causes emotional and sometimes physical pain. Punishment diminishes the power of the recipient, who typically blames the punisher for causing the problem and does not view himself or herself as being in a position to solve it. The punisher is viewed as the one with the power to control behavior, and the recipient of punishment sees no reason to engage in self-evaluation, a strategy critical to choosing responsible behavior. As noted previously, the use of extrinsic rewards is also a way to obtain compliance. Thus, as in the use of punishment, the person administering the rewards is viewed as having the power to control behavior, and the recipient of the reward also sees no reason to engage in behavioral self-evaluation.

Discipline, on the other hand, helps promote self-evaluation of behavior. By learning to behave consistently in an acceptable manner, one earns freedom because those with the authority to manage choices trust that acceptable choices will be made and appropriate actions will follow. The more learners are in effective control of their behavior, the more powerful they feel. The more successful they are in choosing acceptable behaviors, the more likely they are to be engaged by others who behave appropriately. As a result, life in school becomes more need fulfilling and pleasurable. The learner grows in self-confidence and self-esteem, and becomes increasingly able to participate creatively and constructively in classroom and school activities.[15] School becomes a part of the learner's quality world. The learner increases his or her capacity to evaluate personal behavior, especially by addressing the questions "What do I need?" "Is what I am doing likely to get me what I need?" and "Is my behavioral choice fair to others?"

Sense-based behavior management systems

When the teacher knows that discipline is a positive learning experience based on the learner's self-evaluation and choice, both the self-evaluation of behavior and the generation and evaluation of alternative behavioral choices become basic to successful participation in the classroom. The teacher must develop a plan to engage learners in activities that promote responsibility and quality behavior. A *sense-based system* for defining behavioral expectations is fundamental to this plan.

Each learner must fully understand the behavioral expectations of the school and the classroom. Such understanding is simplified when those expectations make sense to the learner. Expectations make sense when there is a logical, age-appropriate explanation for their existence; when rules are few and simple; when expectations are predictable and can be applied to new situations; and when the consequences for inappropriate behavior are known, nonpunitive, and consistently applied. The rights and responsibilities concept presented in this chapter is understandable to students because it is based on a logical system of thought—a system that also happens to be fundamental to our democratic traditions. Rules within such a framework simply serve to let everyone know his or her responsibilities and safeguard the rights of all: In other words, rules make explicit the relationship between responsibilities and rights. Such a logical and fundamentally simple notion provides students with a framework they can use even without adult intervention to determine what is and what is not acceptable behavior. This type of independent assessment is crucial to the development of responsible behavior. In brief, the sense-based system for determining acceptable and unacceptable behavior reduces rule confusion and concerns regarding the uniform enforcement of rules.

A *rule-abundant system* is the antithesis of the sense-based approach. Most schools, in fact most of our institutions, are, however, rule-abundant systems. In a rule-abundant system, the various rules are, or at least appear to be, unconnected and unrelated. Rules are many and complex, behavioral expectations are not easily applied to new situations, and the consequences for inappropriate behavior—usually punitive—are neither understandable nor consistently applied. In such a system, rules proliferate with each new problem because those in charge of the system depend on rules to solve problems (i.e., conflicts). These rules become sacred, often more important than the problems they were designed to solve. The abundance of rules results because each crisis usually requires more than one rule to resolve. Often the need for the extra rules becomes apparent only when the original rule is challenged by those whose behavior it was intended to control. Because rules are generated to address a specific crisis, often there is no rational, systematic basis for them as a whole.

It is not much of a stretch to conclude that a significant number of conflicts in schools occur because of confusion regarding behavioral expectations and rules. When expectations are unclear, one learner is likely to attempt to satisfy a basic need in a way that thwarts another peer's or an adult's attempt to satisfy a basic need. Even if the learner knows all the rules, he or she may still feel unjustly singled out. Complaints like "But Susie did the same thing, and she wasn't punished" or "I was just doing what I've been told to do when John picked on me. Why don't you reprimand John?" are common.

Under a sense-based system, questions such as "What right did you violate?" "Do you think anyone's rights were denied in this situation?" "Did you exercise your responsibility?" and "Did you do so the best you know how to do?" serve as facilitative probes to help the learner evaluate his or her own behavior in a context of reason and logic rather than in the context of adult authority. It is difficult for a learner to evaluate his or her own behavior when rules seem arbitrary and the justification is "because I (the adult) said so." From the child's viewpoint, the rules of the system almost always exist without justification. It is the adult's responsibility to provide the justification. "Because I said so" is probably insufficient justification for most young people today. Table 5.4 contrasts the main characteristics of a sense-based behavior management system with those of a rule-abundant system.

Clearly, the goals of the school to develop responsible learners and future citizens will best be served if any rules created are sensible and generalizable. Students cannot choose responsible behaviors or resolve behavioral conflicts within a system without behavioral norms. When the authority and justification for rules are the exclusive domain of the adults in the system, students are unlikely to be successful in choosing alternative behaviors or in unassisted conflict resolution.

Rights and responsibilities

To build the foundation for learners to make responsible behavioral choices in the classroom and school, and to develop a culture where human dignity and self-esteem are valued, all individuals must understand their basic human rights, respect those rights for self and others, and learn how to exercise their rights without infringing upon the rights of others. Teaching respect for human rights and the responsibilities associated with those rights begins with the adoption of rights and responsibilities to govern the school and the classrooms in it. These rights and responsibilities become the constitution under which the rules and conventions of management and interaction are generated.

Rights are guaranteed conditions—privileges or freedoms that are given to everyone all the time. They are what one should always expect. *Responsibilities* are something one is always expected to do, a way one is always expected to act, and a way one is expected to treat someone else. There is a simple and direct relationship between rights and responsibilities in any social context:

Table 5.4

Characteristics of Sense-Based versus Rule-Abundant Behavior Management Systems

Sense-based system	Rule-abundant system
Has a logical organization.	Lacks organization.
Rules are few and simple, predictable, and generalizable.	Rules are many and complex, lack predictability, and cannot be generalized (situation specific).
Consequences for inappropriate behavior are known and consistently applied.	Consequences for inappropriate behavior are unknown and/or inconsistently applied.
Authority derives from the system.	Authority derives from those in charge.
Reduces rule confusion.	Is characterized by rule confusion.

Enjoying a right requires everyone to accept and exercise certain responsibilities. Constructing a rights and responsibilities document that displays the relationship between each right and the related responsibility is a tool for discussing behavioral expectations. Table 5.5 is a prototype of such a document, which may be applied in any setting.

This prototype is only an example; rights and responsibilities likely will vary from place to place. It is important only that the same rights and responsibilities govern all within a given place. Table 5.6 exhibits a document entitled "Leal Rights and Responsibilities," which shows how one school, Leal Elementary School in Urbana, Illinois, stated its behavioral expectations when Richard Bodine served as principal.

In the context of our democratic culture, the notion of rights and related responsibilities makes sense to everyone. These behavioral expectations apply to all members of the school environment—adults or children, teachers or learners.

A school might employ one of the following strategies to develop its rights and responsibilities statement. The composition of the working group that uses the chosen strategy is also likely an important decision. A broad-based consensus of school staff and clientele is ultimately required. Representative involvement in the building process from the outset may be a prudent move to assure that consensus.

One strategy is to approach the task as a step-by-step creative process from an unencumbered perspective. The group or subgroups brainstorm two lists (remember, brainstorming is a generation process that should be free of evaluation):

1. List all the privileges or freedoms that you believe individuals should be able to experience.

2. List all the responsibilities—a way one is always expected to behave; something one is always expected to do—that individuals are expected to perform.

3. Combine the two lists by matching any related rights and responsibilities, using the two-column format exhibited for the prototype (see Table 5.6).

4. List any leftover rights in the left column and generate a responsibility statement for each.

5. List any leftover responsibilities in the right column and generate a rights statement for each.

6. Eliminate any rights or responsibilities that would not apply to everyone.

7. Combine statements where appropriate.

The goal is to have a relatively small number of general statements with broad application. For example, rights and responsibilities for a school apply to the youngest students as well as to the oldest students, apply to the adults as well as to the students. The goal is not to cover every conceivable circumstance, but generally to define expectations for all conceivable circumstances. Rights and responsibilities are not simply rules but a framework under which specific

Table 5.5
Rights and Responsibilities

Rights	Responsibilities
I have the right:	I have the responsibility:
To be treated with respect and kindness: No one will tease me, demean me, or insult me.	To treat all others with respect and kindness by not teasing, demeaning, or insulting them.
To be myself: No one will treat me unfairly due to looks, abilities, beliefs, or gender.	To honor individual differences by treating all others fairly regardless of looks, abilities, beliefs, or gender.
To be safe: No one will threaten me, bully me, or damage or remove my property.	To help make the environment safe by not acting dangerously, and by securing my property, by not threatening or bullying others, and by respecting the property of others.
To be heard: No one will yell at me, and my opinions will be considered.	To listen to others, consider their opinions, and allow others to be heard.
To be free to express my feelings and opinions without criticism and to learn about myself through constructive feedback.	To express myself respectfully in ways others can hear me and to allow others to express themselves and provide constructive feedback.
To learn and to be given assistance to do so.	To accept assistance when given in the spirit of increasing my opportunity to learn and grow, and to unconditionally provide assistance to others whenever I can do so.
To expect that all rights will be mine in all circumstances and to receive assistance from those in charge when that is not the case.	To protect my rights and the rights of others by exercising my full responsibilities at all times and by helping others to do the same.

Table 5.6
Leal Rights and Responsibilities

My rights:	My responsibilities:
I have a right to be happy and to be treated with compassion in this school. This means that no one will laugh at me or hurt my feelings.	I have the responsibility to treat others with compassion. This means that I will not laugh at others, tease others, or try to hurt the feelings of others.
I have the right to be myself in this school. This means that no one will treat me unfairly because I am black or white . . .	I have the responsibility to respect others as individuals and not to treat others unfairly because they are black or white . . .

fat or thin	fat or thin
tall or short	tall or short
boy or girl	boy or girl
adult or child.	adult or child.

I have the right to be safe in this school. This means that no one will . . .	I have the responsibility to make the school safe by not . . .

hit me	hitting anyone
kick me	kicking anyone
push me	pushing anyone
pinch me	pinching anyone
threaten me	threatening anyone
hurt me.	hurting anyone.

I have the right to expect my property to be safe in this school.	I have the responsibility not to take or destroy the property of others.
I have the right to hear and be heard in this school. This means that no one will . . .	I have the responsibility to help maintain a calm and quiet school. This means that I will not . . .

yell	yell
scream	scream
shout	shout
make loud noises	make loud noises
or otherwise disturb me.	or otherwise disturb others.

My rights:

I have the right to learn about myself and others in this school. This means that I will be free to express my feelings and opinions without being interrupted or punished.

I have the right to be helped to learn self-control in this school. This means that no one will silently stand by while I abuse my rights.

I have the right to expect that these rights will be mine in all circumstances so long as I am exercising my full responsibilities.

My responsibilities:

I have the responsibility to learn about myself and others in this school. This means that I will be free to express my feelings and opinions without being interrupted or punished, and I will not interrupt or punish others who express their feelings and opinions.

I have the responsibility to learn self-control in this school. This means that I will strive to exercise my rights without denying the same rights to others, and I will expect to be corrected when I do abuse the rights of others as they shall be corrected if my rights are abused.

I have the responsibility to protect my rights and the rights of others by exercising my full responsibility in all circumstances.

---

rules could fit. Rights and responsibilities are designed to imply behavioral expectations, not to make all behavioral expectations explicit.

Another strategy is to approach the task as a step-by-step process of reconstruction. The group or subgroups examine the school's present discipline policy and behavioral expectations and construct two lists from what is gleaned from the examination— one list written as rights, the other as responsibilities. These two lists are used to complete steps 3 through 7, as just described for the other strategy. If any part of the present discipline policy can- not be reconstructed as rights and responsibilities, that part of the present policy requires further consideration. What remains of the present policy may be specific rules not easily reconstituted as rights and responsibilities. Chapter 6 will deal more fully with rules and how they fit into the management plan.

As stated previously, in a sense-based system, rules make explicit the relationship between rights and responsibilities. For example, many rules tell one what is safe behavior and certainly correlate with the right to be safe and the related responsibility. The common school rule "No running in the halls" is about safe behavior, not about running. When others are present and when another might suddenly open a door in front of you or step into your path, running constitutes a risk to you and others. Running down the middle of the hall when no one else is present is likely not a violation of your or anyone else's right to be safe.

From what remains of your present policy, extract those things that appear to be rules and use the information in the next chapter to transform them into a sense-based system. For any of the present policy that still remains, ask, Why is this necessary? Do we need this? If the answer is no, eliminate that policy. If the answer is yes, you must generate an explanation that will make "sense" to those expected to behave as the policy requires. What will your age-appropriate explanation be for the expected behavior?

Because no student who feels threatened or coerced can engage in quality learning or quality behavior, and because coercion is counterproductive to a cooperative context and is a dysfunctional conflict resolution behavior, the teacher must be unconditionally committed to managing the classroom without coercion. This commitment, enacted within this kind of sense-based behavior management system, is the foundation for the classroom discipline program. This approach to discipline provides a teaching-learning environment that promotes responsible behavioral choice founded on the emerging capabilities of emotional intelligence.

Chapters 6 and 7 present additional information for developing pragmatic action plans for creating responsible learners in our schools and responsible citizens for our world.

Endnotes

1. A. Kohn, "Beyond Discipline," *Education Week* 20 November (1996), 37.

2. P. Salovey and J. Mayer, "Emotional Intelligence," *Imagination, Cognition, and Personality 9* (1990).

3. D. Goleman, *Emotional Intelligence* (New York: Bantam Books, 1995), 289–290.

4. Goleman, *Emotional Intelligence.*

5. H. Weisinger, *Emotional Intelligence at Work* (San Francisco: Jossey-Bass, 1998), 6.

6. W. Glasser, *Control Theory in the Classroom* (New York: Harper and Row, 1986).

7. Glasser, *Control Theory in the Classroom.*

8. Goleman, *Emotional Intelligence.*

9. W. J. Kreidler, *Conflict Resolution in the Middle School* (Cambridge, MA: Educators for Social Responsibility, 1994).

10. R. J. Bodine, D. K. Crawford, and F. Schrumpf, *Creating the Peaceable School: A Comprehensive Program for Teaching Conflict Resolution* (Champaign, IL: Research Press, 1994).

11. D. W. Johnson and R. T. Johnson, "Cooperative Learning and Conflict Resolution," *The Fourth R 42* (1993), 1.

12. Bodine et al., *Creating the Peaceable School.*

13. Johnson and Johnson, "Cooperative Learning."

14. Bodine et al., *Creating the Peaceable School,* 16–17.

15. Bodine et al., *Creating the Peaceable School.*

CHAPTER 6

How to Manage the Classroom for Emotional Intelligence

A healthy, positive school and classroom climate is critical for developing emotional intelligence in everyone. Key components of school climate are the overall behavioral expectations held for the learners and the manner in which the adult managers establish, facilitate the internalization of, and enforce those expectations. Necessary conditions are a school consensus for a responsibility education program based on commonly accepted behavioral expectations and procedures that assure that each learner has the opportunity and support necessary to internalize acceptable behaviors. The classroom teacher has the ultimate responsibility for promoting acceptable and successful behaviors from every learner, including accessing support services from others when the learner, for whatever reason, is not experiencing success. Support services may be for the teacher, for the learner, or for both teacher and learner. The teacher's efforts alone may be insufficient for every learner, but the teacher's efforts are always an essential component of the support system for each learner. The ultimate success of efforts to develop emotional intelligence rests in the teacher's ability and willingness to form a caring, supportive relationship with each learner. In nearly all of the literature on resiliency in youth, it is commonly held that each young person needs, in order to survive and grow, at least one adult who unconditionally cares about him or her. Who better to do that in schools than a teacher?

Management practices designed to promote responsible behavior must forsake the coercive strategies of punishments and rewards in favor of discipline. Responsible behavior is generated through

111

expectations and support, not through directives, orders, or demands (the precursors of punishment) nor through the subterfuge of rewards. The teacher transfers responsibility to the learner for choosing behaviors that fit within the established acceptable standards not through force, domination, or trickery, but through reason and facilitative assistance. This facilitative assistance enables the learner to self-evaluate his or her behavior regarding the following ambient factors:

- The precise nature of the current total behavior, focusing especially on the action component of that total behavior

- The purpose of the current chosen behavior in relation to the learner's basic psychological needs of belonging, power, freedom, and fun

- The degree to which the current behavior provides for or has the potential to provide for satisfaction of the learner's basic psychological needs

- The impact or potential impact of the chosen behavior upon the rights of others in the community (classroom or school)

This facilitative assistance also enables the learner to explore and plan alternative behavior whenever the self-evaluation determines the current behavior to be insufficient.

Responsibility Education

The teacher who manages the classroom for emotional intelligence understands the necessity of communicating high expectations regarding both learning and behavior. The teacher also realizes that it is impossible to elicit learning and behavior simply by declaring that they are desired and expected. The teacher approaches the development and use of quality behavior as proactively as he or she approaches the development of quality learning. The teacher knows that discipline is a positive learning experience based on the learner's self-evaluation and choice.

The teacher, therefore, is required to develop a plan to engage learners in activities that promote responsibility education and quality behavior. The first step is to make sure that each learner fully understands the behavioral expectations of the school and of the classroom. It is unfair to expect people to behave in any manner other than how they have been taught to behave. If the school has not taught the behavior, where might we assume that it was taught to all learners? The classroom is, must be, the forum for such teaching. Is it fair to exclaim, at the exhibition of unwanted behavior, "You should know better than that"?

The teaching program for responsible behavior involves two broad parameters. First, what constitutes acceptable and unacceptable behavior is delineated and explained to learners in an age-appropriate manner, including a rationale that makes sense to the learner. Second, for unacceptable behavior, alternate acceptable behaviors are identified, and the connections between basic need satisfaction and the alternative behaviors are made conspicuous.

The process of learning behavioral expectations and constraints is facilitated when these are consistent throughout the school. The development of rights and responsibilities for the school (chapter 5) provides a school constitution for responsible behavior. Staff consensus on such a document is the first step. Staff agreement on a process for educating learners about the rights and responsibilities is also needed. Simply having a constitution in place does virtually nothing unless there is a concerted effort to inform and educate about its meanings and implications. Each teacher has the responsibility to engage his or her students in discussions and activities designed to enable the learners to understand the concepts of rights and responsibilities and how the expectations and rules of the school reflect these concepts. Class meetings, described later in this chapter, are one way to do this.

In addition to the general school constitution—rights and responsibilities—it is prudent to develop staff consensus on the most highly undesirable behaviors, those the school would target to extinguish. These select few behaviors, whether presently exhibited or not, would have a profoundly negative impact on the school climate. Although these behaviors may differ from school to school, most schools probably could focus on some or all of the following objectionable behaviors: (a) fighting or attacking, (b) stealing and property defacing or destruction, (c) intimidation or extortion, (d) harassment, (e) aggressive acts toward school employees, and so forth. The school should have a plan involving all available resources to deal with the selected behaviors consistently and at every occurrence. The plan for doing so should be clearly communicated to all learners and all constituents.

Rules for Rules

Targeting highly undesirable behaviors will likely give rise to some specific rules governing behavior. A rule is a statement that either attempts to clarify the relationship between a right and a responsibility or to emphasize the importance of a particular responsibility. To be consistent with the management plan advocated here, rules generated must meet certain conditions:

A rule must make sense to those expected to abide by it and must fit under the general purview of the school constitution (i.e., rights and responsibilities). The rights and responsibilities provide the justification for rules. Whenever a rule is generated that might appear to students to be an exception to the constitution, an age-appropriate, sensible reason for the rule is required. Either a link to the rights and responsibilities is provided, or some other sensible justification is given.

There should be few rules. No one, especially children, can remember many rules. Many rules are implicit in the rights and responsibility document. Specific rules are needed only to emphasize the seriousness of a behavior or to cover conditions not inherent in the rights and responsibilities. When an additional rule appears needed, determine whether a present rule can be eliminated. Perhaps a rule has achieved its purpose and no longer needs to be emphasized.

A rule is stated in the positive. Rules are more effective and meaningful when they describe desired rather than undesired behavior. A rule actually defines or describes behavior. Why would we want to define or describe unwanted behavior? Might that suggest a behavior to someone that he or she had not yet thought of?

A rule must be enforceable. A rule is useless unless it can be enforced in all circumstances in which it applies, regardless of the individuals involved in the circumstance. Consistency in the management of behavior is paramount. Unenforceable rules or selective enforcement of rules creates confusion regarding expectations. When a rule is not consistently applied, a significant number of individuals may be willing to risk not following the rule. If the rule is then enforced with those individuals, they can and will claim unfair treatment.

Rules are not sacred. A rule can be, must be, changed if it is not working to create the desired sense of community.

Breaking a rule results in a consequence. In the management system advocated here, the logical consequence that is always applicable in all circumstances for each individual is the requirement to choose another behavior that is acceptable within the social context—a responsible behavior. If it is deemed, through the consensus process of constructing the management system, that additional consequences are appropriate, those consequences must not be punitive or coercive. They also must be logical consequences. The characteristics of logical consequences are as follows:

1. They are known in advance. The rule and the consequence for not following the rule are clearly linked and that link has been explained. The axiom is "If you choose not to follow the rule, you choose the consequence." If it is clearly communicated that choosing to fight at school results in a suspension of school privileges when one fights, one chooses the suspension when one chooses to fight. This clear relationship facilitates the questioning process "What are you doing?" and "What are you choosing when you do that?"

2. They do not cause actual physical pain and do not involve public humiliation. Logical consequences respond to the misbehavior in ways that preserve the behaver's dignity—the behavior is the problem, not the person exhibiting the behavior.

3. They are related to the problem behavior. A logical consequence reinforces an acceptable behavior. For example, the requirement to clean graffiti from a bathroom wall is related

to drawing the graffiti on the wall. It also reinforces respect for public property.

As for the development of the rights and responsibilities document described in chapter 5, two strategies exist for identifying the targeted problem behaviors and generating the rules needed to communicate the importance of behaving appropriately in these arenas. The creative process from the unencumbered perspective is to brainstorm problem behaviors and then to prioritize the four or five to be targeted. The reconstruction strategy might involve examining that part of the present discipline policy that does not fit into the rights and responsibilities framework. Is the leftover part necessary? If yes, what is the justification? Does the leftover policy focus on behaviors to target? Are these the four or five most important behaviors to target?

It is important to acknowledge that schools are a part of a larger community/society. That which is clearly illegal in the larger community/society is also illegal in school; therefore, schools do not need their own rules about possession of illegal substances or drugs or weapons. Legal consequences exist for such behaviors; schools should involve community resources and authorities whenever these behaviors are manifested in the school.

A consensus agreement among the staff is also required regarding what constitutes acceptable learner behavior and what strategies to employ to help learners display acceptable behavior. This consensus is built upon the notion that each learner is doing the best the learner knows how to do to meet his or her basic psychological needs for belonging, power, freedom, and fun. If, in the judgment of the adults in the school, the learner's behavior is unacceptable, the adults are responsible for assisting the learner, through the self-evaluation/planning process of reality therapy (chapter 4), to choose an acceptable behavior.

The school rights and responsibilities, consensus about unacceptable behaviors, consensus regarding acceptable behaviors, and the strategies to use to help learners display such behaviors provide a framework for the behavior management system. Everyone is unified by these behavioral expectations at all times. Once the basic framework is agreed upon, strategies are developed to inform learners of the expectations and to assist each in understanding them. These strategies will of necessity involve interactions with both groups of learners, perhaps the entire class in class meeting discussions, and with individual learners who need additional assistance in choosing new behavior. These discussions, especially group discussions in the format of class meetings, are scheduled regularly and constitute the most important element of the social and emotional education program of the school and classroom. The discussions are designed to help learners gain understanding about their behavior and the effect that behavior has on others. Learners are also exposed to alternative behaviors. Failure of the entire school to devote adequate time to the process of social education will result in a school characterized by discipline concerns. Behavior problems will largely be the result of individuals attempting to do the best they know how to do in situations where they are either uncertain as to what is expected or where they believe the expectations to be unreasonable and capricious. Individuals will follow a rule if it is known and if it is seen as in their best interest—that is, it is need satisfying.

The behavior management program for developing emotional intelligence includes educational strategies for promoting responsible behavior (creating a vision of quality behavior) and intervention strategies for helping the individual learners achieve quality behavior. Specific components of the program are as follows:

- Class meetings
- Life rules
- C. A. R. E. time (Communication About Responsibility Education)
- Time-out

These components and the conflict resolution processes presented in chapter 7 promote understanding of the guidelines for behavior in the learning environment and provide the teacher and the learner with processes for solving problems by planning for different behaviors. This program is designed to ensure that all learners will be engaged in quality learning and that they will not disrupt the learning opportunities of others—that is, they will practice responsible behavior.

Class Meetings

The class meeting can be a most effective vehicle for responsibility education. Although meetings are time consuming, they are critical to the success of the classroom in promoting the development of emotional intelligence and responsible behavior. As a rule, such meetings require considerable time during the early weeks of the school term, as this is the time for orientation, teaching, and reteaching. However, the real payoff comes when meetings are scheduled regularly throughout the school term. Meeting activities are consistent with the desired learner outcomes of the responsibility education program. The activities provide a systematic way for learners to gain an understanding of and respect for self and others, to develop an understanding of behavior and of conflict, and to develop the social problem solving skills they will need in life. These are outcomes learners will not realize unless they have opportunities to explore behavioral alternatives and practice problem solving. Learners of every age experience difficulties in getting along with one another and find interpersonal problems most difficult to solve. Without help resolving these difficulties, "learners tend to evade the problems, to lie their way out of situations, to depend on others to solve their problems, or just to give up. None of these courses of action is good preparation for life."[1] None is the behavior of an effective citizen.

Class meetings have the following functions in the behavior management context:

1. They introduce the behavioral expectations and help learners understand the reasons for the rules in the social setting.

2. They help learners understand their basic psychological needs and wants as well as the choices they can make to get their needs met.

3. They help learners understand diversity, conflicts, and problems.

4. They provide a forum for addressing individual and group educational and behavioral problems at both classroom and school levels. (Group problem solving, described in chapter 7, is a specialized use of the class meeting.)

5. They help learners discover that they have both individual and group responsibilities for learning and for behaving in a way that fosters a sense of community.

6. They help learners understand that, although the world may be difficult and may at times appear hostile and mysterious, they can use their minds to solve the problems of living in their world.

7. They help learners see the relevance of the expected school and classroom behavior to behavioral expectations in real-life settings.[2]

Problems affecting the class as a whole, as well as particular problems affecting individual members, may be eligible for discussion, although the teacher and class should establish ground rules governing the introduction of an individual problem that is not directly school related. The group discussion should always be focused on the issue. If the meeting is for group problem solving, it is directed toward solving the problem, and the solution should never include punishment or fault finding. If class meetings are held with some frequency, participants will become aware that many problems are not amenable to quick solutions: Some have no single best solution, and some have a best solution that is only a "lesser evil." If problem identification is an open group process, there is little danger that only those problems with a clear solution will be chosen for discussion.

The following questions and statements, in no particular order, may be used in class meetings to promote general understanding of rights and responsibilities, expectations, and their connecting relationships. Other discussion topics for class meetings are included in the appendix.

1. What is responsibility?

2. Give examples of occasions when you felt you exhibited responsible behavior.

3. Can you give an example of a situation in which someone else behaved in a manner that you thought was responsible?

4. Describe an action you have taken that you are proud of.

5. What is "right"?

6. What is "wrong"?

7. How do you decide right or wrong?

8. How might you help someone who is having difficulty following the rules? How could someone help you?

9. Describe something someone else did that made you feel proud of him or her.

10. What does freedom mean?

11. What is a friend?

12. What would you like to change about yourself?

13. What would you not like to have to change about yourself?

14. What motivates you to do your best?

15. Who understands you?

16. How do you feel about yourself?

17. How do you think others see you?

18. Whom do you understand?

19. Describe your most cherished freedom.

20. What is a freedom (privilege) you do not now have that you would like to have?

21. What is cooperation? What is competition?

22. Give examples of occasions when you or someone else showed cooperative behavior.

23. How do you feel when you compete and win? Compete and lose?

24. Is cooperation ever harmful? Is competition ever harmful?

25. Describe situations or activities where you believe cooperation would not be helpful.

26. When is competition essential?

27. What is conflict?

28. What do you usually do when you find yourself in conflict with a peer? With an adult?

29. What do you want when your are in conflict with another person?

30. Does what you do when you are in a conflict with another usually help you get what you want? Why? Why not?[3]

The class meeting is an appropriate forum for reviewing the school rights and responsibilities as well as any related rules and the reasons behind those rules. It is also a forum for discussing the consequences of not following the rules, helping an individual or the group determine alternative behaviors to replace unacceptable ones, suggesting strategies to help an individual deal with someone who is creating a problem for him or her, and exploring a variety of ways to meet expectations. The class meeting can be a vehicle for generating expectations for the classroom—in other words, class rules.

Life Rules

The next stage in the process of constructing the management system is to engage the learners in activities to help them understand the specific rules that govern behavior in their various classrooms. Obviously, classroom expectations must be congruent with those of the school, and discussions and other learning activities should be designed to help learners see the relationship between the two sets of expectations. Each classroom teacher develops any specific rules that might be needed because of, for example, special classroom circumstance (a gym class, a science lab, a machine shop, etc.) or special population circumstance, dictating that a rule be stated age appropriately (a kindergarten class, a class for mentally challenged learners, a program for severely emotionally challenged students, etc.). Any specific rules generated for specific locales within the school should meet the same conditions for rules described previously in this chapter. To summarize, special attention should be paid to the following:

- A rule is stated in the positive.
- There are few rules.
- A rule must make sense to those expected to abide by it.
- A rule must be enforceable.
- A rule should help create the desired sense of community.

- Breaking the rule results in a consequence—a different behavior is expected.

With the rights and responsibilities constitution in place, the teacher as manager is in a position to establish expectations for work and behavior in the learning environment. Because the rights and responsibilities provide a framework to do so, learners can participate in establishing those expectations and will therefore have ownership. For example, an expectation for work may state that learners may choose learning activities to pursue; they may not elect to do nothing. An expectation for behavior might be that when a fellow learner asks for help, you should provide whatever assistance you can. Such expectations, as simple and few as possible, are designed to guarantee that all learners will be engaged fully in learning activities and that each will contribute actively to building the community of learners within the classroom. The teacher is responsible for promoting acceptable and successful behaviors from every learner. Each learner is expected to strive for quality—to do the best he or she can do and be the best he or she can be.

Rules for the school and the classroom are the rules for success in any life venture. Helping learners make this connection is the ultimate goal of the responsibility education program. One possible focus for classroom expectations could be on *life rules*. The teacher could orchestrate a discussion of behavior expected in the real world that allows people to succeed and to get their needs satisfied. For example, when adults are responsible, prompt, prepared, participate, and show respect, their chances for success and satisfaction increase. Once these life rules are identified, the teacher facilitates discussions and activities designed to enable the class to translate each rule into a desired classroom behavior (see Table 6.1).

Rules need to be flexible to accommodate genuine mitigating circumstances. Life rules are rarely rigid. For example, in real life, there are probably few absolute deadlines. Generally a deadline can be extended so a quality result will be obtained. Even the Internal Revenue Service allows an extension to a taxpayer who meets minimum requirements. The life rules of the school and the classroom also must be reasonably flexible. The goal is to help learners learn the value of life rules. People of all ages tend to follow rules that enable them to get along and be safe. For example, games require

---

Table 6.1
Life Rules Translated into Classroom Behaviors

Life rules	Classroom behaviors
Prompt	Meeting deadlines
Prepared	Having materials
	Listening for instructions
	Following directions
Participate	Being a part of discussion
	Completing work
	Staying engaged
Respect	Honoring self and others
	Valuing property
Responsible	Accepting ownership
	Planning more effective behavior

---

rules that let all players play in the same manner to achieve a meaningful outcome; traffic signs enable drivers to travel with greater safety and a minimum of fear. The real reason a driver stops at a stop sign is not the possible consequence of getting a ticket, but the belief that stopping is in the driver's best interest and in the interest of others. A consequence in and of itself will not change a behavior. A consequence only works when learners find value in the relationship with the person asking them to do something, or when they see value in what they are being asked to do.

Life rules are one "sense-based" foundation for rules—the rules make sense because valid reasons for them exist. Whatever validating base is selected, adherence to the "rules for rules" is strategic. Involvement of learners in the creation of these rules for specific circumstances provides them a sense of ownership and solidifies understanding of the necessity for and the desirability of the rules.

By providing regular and meaningful opportunities to consider responsibility and quality behavior, largely through whole-class activities such as the class meeting, the teacher enables learners in formulating a picture of quality behavior that can become a part of their quality world. For most learners, these group opportunities are sufficient to internalize quality behaviors. These learners generally have a success identity. They are in control of their lives and, given clear, sensible parameters, will choose effective behaviors to satisfy their psychological needs. On those occasions when their behavior choices create problems for themselves or for others, they will accept responsibility for planning different behaviors. They believe they will succeed.

Others, however, will need additional attention and support from the teacher, and perhaps other adults in the school, to understand the expectations and to learn the behaviors that are consistent with those expectations. These learners need varying degrees of assistance through the discipline program to become aware that internalizing quality behaviors will be personally need satisfying. These are generally the learners who have a failure identity. They are not in effective control of their lives, and when their behavior choices create problems for themselves or for others, they do not easily accept responsibility for planning different behaviors. They believe they will fail and that what they are now doing is the only thing they can do. For these individuals, the teacher and perhaps other adults may need to establish a counseling environment and employ the procedures that lead to change presented in chapter 4. These individuals present the most challenge to any management system, yet they are the very individuals who most require noncoercive interventions.

Ultimately, the teacher establishes a personal relationship with the learner, causes the learner to focus on the doing component of his or her present behavior, facilitates the learner through the self-evaluation process to conclude that the present behavior is not need fulfilling, helps the learner develop a plan for a different behavior, and obtains a commitment from the learner to behave according to the plan. Importantly, in circumstances where the individual does not succeed in implementing the plan, the teacher neither reverts to punishment nor accepts excuses. When this happens, the teacher reengages the learner in the procedures that lead to change. Punishment breaks the personal relationship requisite for the entire procedure, and so does accepting excuses. Accepting excuses often seems humane, and the learner may seek this acceptance, often aggressively. But accepting excuses also breaks the relationship. The learner understands that his or her behavior is not quality behavior, and when the teacher accepts excuses for something less than the learner's best, the learner will conclude that the teacher really does not care. Would a person who cares accept excuses while another messes up his or her life? Students with a failure identity do not change behavior easily or quickly. It is highly likely that such learners will not succeed in carrying out their plans. The real danger in accepting excuses for inappropriate behavior or inferior work is in the message such acceptance sends to the learner. The message, perhaps unintended, is "You are worthless." The learner's translation is "You don't care." The teacher who refuses to accept excuses is saying, "You are a worthwhile person, and I am waiting for you to complete your commitment." For example, if an assignment is not completed, rather than say, "Why didn't you do it?" the teacher should say, "When will you do it?" "Can you do it?" "Can you do it in school today?" "After school?"[4] Or, when a behavior is unacceptable, rather than say, "Stop doing that!" the teacher should say, "What are you doing?" "Are you following our rules for this classroom?" "Can you choose to do something different?" "Will you choose a different behavior?" A simple protocol for the noncoercive manager is, whenever you are inclined to give an order, command, or directive, ask a question instead. Instead of saying, "Listen to me," ask "What is your responsibility when another is speaking?"

School discipline is problematic because administrators and teachers not only deal with a large variety of excuses for inappropriate behavior—some individual and some group excuses—they also ask for those excuses. Discipline is poorly understood; thus, behavior management is poorly understood. Discipline has nothing to do with hurting or harming learners. Rather, it is helping learners first to realize that their current behaviors are not enabling them to meet their needs and then helping them choose more successful, need-fulfilling behaviors. Discipline is education. It takes learners a long time to fulfill commitments, especially the commitment to quality learning and responsible behavior.

The next two components of the noncoercive behavior management program provide two different ways to help learners take effective control of their behavior. *C.A.R.E. time* is used when a student is not producing quality work or following work guidelines, and *time-out* is used with the student who is disrupting the learning environment of others.

C.A.R.E. Time

C.A.R.E. (Communication About Responsibility Education) time is a brief period for the teacher and the learner to communicate about completion of work and engagement in classroom activities. This communication can be woven into the teacher's and learner's natural interactions within the classroom setting, or it can occur at a scheduled time during or outside the learner's school day. The primary purpose of C.A.R.E. time is to help learners focus on how they are acting, thinking, and feeling, and on what they want; evaluate whether their chosen behaviors are helping them get their needs met effectively; and develop and commit to plans for effective, quality behavior.

During C.A.R.E. time, the teacher poses questions such as the following.

What are you doing? Focus on total behaviors—that is, how the learner is thinking, acting, and feeling. Help the learner understand that all behaviors are chosen. Other probes are:

- Describe what you are doing.
- What are you thinking?
- What do you do when you think that way?
- What choices did you make?
- How are you spending your time?
- What are the directions?
- What is our rule that applies to this situation?

What do you want? Focus on the learner's present picture and expand it to the learner's quality world—the way he or she wants life to be. Other probes are:

- What do you really want?
- How would you like things to be?

- How do you want this class/school to be?
- What would you like to happen?
- What do you want from me? From others?
- What don't you want?
- Are you seeking to belong?
- Do you want to be successful?
- Do you want recognition?
- Do you want to be in control?

Is the present behavior going to get you what you want? Focus on getting the learner to evaluate his or her behavior. Other probes are:

- Is what you are doing helping you get what you want?
- Is it possible to get what you want?
- How is this helping you?
- Are you following the rules?
- Are you satisfied with your effort/achievement/performance?
- Is it important for you to be successful?
- Is your behavior a responsible choice to protect your rights? Others' rights?
- Is what you are doing helping you feel better about yourself?
- Is this behavior drawing others to you?
- Are you having fun?

What can you do to get what you want? Focus on developing a plan that has a good chance of success. Other probes are:

- Can you choose a different behavior?
- Can you follow our rule?
- What's your job now?
- Do you want to figure out a better way?
- What can I do to help you so you can _____?

The following dialogues between teachers and learners illustrate how C.A.R.E. time can be used.

C.A.R.E. TIME SCENARIO 1

Teacher: *Diana, have you finished the book report?*[25]

Diana: *No.*

Teacher: *What are you doing?*

Diana: *Nothing.*

Teacher: *You are doing something. What are you doing?*

Diana: *I am listening to Tonya and Jason talk.*

Teacher: *Is listening to Tonya and Jason right now helping you finish your book report that is due today?*

Diana: *Probably not. No, I guess it isn't.*

Teacher: *What do you want?*

Diana: *What do you mean?*

Teacher: *Do you want to be a successful learner in this class, a learner who does quality work?*

Diana: *Yes.*

Teacher: *Remember the life rule to be prompt. Is not finishing assignments on time going to help you be a successful person?*

Diana: *No, I guess not.*

Teacher: *Do you want to be a successful person?*

Diana: *Well, of course. Yes.*

Teacher: *What can you do now to get what you want?*

Diana: *I can go to the reading center and finish my report now.*

Teacher: *Will you do that?*

Diana: *Yes.*

C.A.R.E. TIME SCENARIO 2

Teacher: *Andrew, are you working on the exercise?*

Andrew: *Yeah.*

Teacher:	*What were you just doing?*
Andrew:	*I was passing a note to Dan.*
Teacher:	*What do you want when you come to school?*
Andrew:	*I want to do well so I can get a good job.*
Teacher:	*You want to perform well in school because you believe doing so will expand your employment opportunities once you graduate. Is that right?*
Andrew:	*I think so.*
Teacher:	*Will passing notes to Dan improve your performance in school?*
Andrew:	*I guess not.*
Teacher:	*What can you do to perform better in school?*
Andrew:	*I can stop passing notes to Dan and concentrate more on the work.*
Teacher:	*Can you do that?*
Andrew:	*Sure.*

C.A.R.E. Time Scenario 3

Teacher:	*Amy, did you finish the morning math assignment?*
Amy:	*No.*
Teacher:	*What are you doing?*
Amy:	*Nothing.*
Teacher:	*What is our rule for work periods?*
Amy:	*We will choose to do something.*
Teacher:	*What did you choose?*
Amy:	*I'm choosing to sit with head down.*
Teacher:	*Are you choosing that behavior for a reason? Are you not feeling well?*
Amy:	*I'm OK. Just a little tired.*
Teacher:	*What do you want?*
Amy:	*I want to get a good grade in this class so my parents can be proud of me and I can ask them to relax some of their rules.*

Teacher:	You want good grades so your parents can be proud of you. What rules do you want relaxed?
Amy:	I want them to trust me and let me have more freedom about what time to be home.
Teacher:	Are you likely to get good grades by sitting through class with your head on your desk?
Amy:	No, I won't, because I'll miss the work you do in class.
Teacher:	What can you do to pay attention during class and get better grades?
Amy:	I can try to keep my head up and not go to sleep during class.
Teacher:	OK. What else can you do?
Amy:	I can try to sleep more at night by turning off MTV earlier.
Teacher:	Do you think you can do those things?
Amy:	I'll try. Yeah, I think I can . . .

It is important to keep in mind that the learner who fails to complete work often sees no purpose for completing the work other than to avoid unpleasant consequences. Thus, work completion becomes a compliant behavior, not a need-fulfilling behavior. When compliance is the reason for completing work, work will rarely be of quality, nor will it be done consistently.

Even when learners see relevance to the work in progress and truly want to do well, they may fail to meet agreed-upon deadlines. This situation requires feedback and counseling from the teacher. Learners typically miss deadlines because they lack experience with time management, underestimating either the time required to complete the activity or the scope of the job—it is more complicated/detailed than assumed. Learners may also underestimate quality—they do not fully visualize the goal (a quality product) until the learning activity is well underway. Self-evaluation and planning during C.A.R.E. time will help the learner become a more efficient time manager.

The convention should exist that either the teacher or the learner may request C.A.R.E. time. Students need to know that frustration is a part of learning and that it is permissible and advisable to request a conference with the teacher for help in addressing the problem.

Time-Out

The primary purpose of time-out is to remove the learner temporarily from a situation where he or she is disrupting the learning environment of others. It is not intended as punishment. Self-evaluation is the only way to promote long-term change in learner behavior. When used properly, time-out will encourage the learner to self-evaluate and make better behavioral choices. When used effectively, the process follows a sports analogy: As in sports, school time-out is used to break the momentum, evaluate the situation, and formulate a plan. The message should be "Something is out of sync, and we need to work it out." The plan that the learner develops in time-out emphasizes the positive behavior that he or she is willing to engage in when the learning activity is resumed—for example, "I will do my work and not disrupt others who are working" or "I'll keep my hands and feet to myself."

Time-out is effective only when the learner and the teacher perceive it as a favorable method for working out problems. If this is to happen, both the classroom and the time-out atmosphere must be positive and noncoercive. Time-out is, in essence, an opportunity for the learner to evaluate his or her behaviors. It is a process that enables the learner to determine that he or she is responsible for behavioral choices. In addition, time-out gives the learner a chance to develop the skills for making more effective behavioral choices—to construct a behavioral plan and commit to act upon that plan.

The time-out location should be comfortable and conducive to problem solving. It may be an area of a classroom or another, separate place in the school. When taking time-out, the learner needs a place to become calm, think about the situation, and develop a plan to return to classroom activities. The duration of the time-out should be up to the learner. The teacher may set a minimum time to avoid further disruption of classroom activities, but ideally the learner returns to the group when he or she has an acceptable plan of action. Very often, the punitive feature of time-out is the fixed time. The idea should be to keep the learner in class and engaged in learning activities, not to interrupt his or her education.

Time-out is, in a sense, a last resort when a behavior problem occurs in the classroom. The preferred approach is for the teacher to ask questions to encourage the learner to evaluate his or her behavior on the spot. The questions focus the learner's attention on the behavior. The teacher can ask one question and continue with other classroom activities, perhaps without waiting for a verbal response. The intent is to have the learner answer the question for himself or herself. It is very difficult for the learner to avoid thinking about the question. The number and types of questions the teacher asks are determined by the severity of behavior, the activity underway, the learner involved, and so on. The tone of the questioning must always be noncoercive. The questions reinforce that the ultimate consequence of inappropriate behavior is the requirement to choose and exhibit an appropriate behavior. Responsible behavior is a condition of participation in the community. The following specific questions are helpful.

To identify the expected and/or target behavior:

- What are you doing?
- What are the directions?
- Can you work on your own?
- Could you please find a space to work on your own?
- Are you following our rules?
- What choice did you make?
- How are you spending your time?
- Is there something I could do to help you?

If the learner continues the unacceptable behavior:

- What is the rule about (specific behavior being challenged)?
- Are you following our rule about this?
- Is what you're doing against the rules?
- How is this helping you?

If the learner still does not stop the unacceptable behavior:

- Are you choosing time-out?

- Do you know what you need to do to stay in this classroom?

- Will you do it?

If the disruptive behavior continues after two or three in-class questioning interventions, it is best to talk briefly with the learner in private. If that isn't possible, the learner should go to the classroom time-out area. To end the time-out and return to classroom activities, the learner must formulate an action plan. The plan may be either verbal or written, depending on the skill and ability of the student and the preference of the teacher.

Verbal Plan

The learner unobtrusively signals the teacher that he or she has a plan and would like to rejoin the group. As soon as possible the teacher goes to the time-out area and asks what the plan is. If the plan is acceptable, the learner returns to the classroom activities: If not, the learner stays in time-out to develop another plan. If possible, the teacher should talk with the learner about the plan. It is especially useful to relate the learner's plan—acceptable or unacceptable—to the behavior that triggered the time-out. A good way to do this is by asking questions, often the same questions asked before the learner was sent to time-out.

Written Plan

If the student has the skills to write a plan and the teacher prefers that approach, forms for these plans may be kept in the time-out area. (See the sample form on the next page.) The learner must complete the planning form before signaling the teacher and returning to classroom activities. The teacher should approve the plan and, if possible, discuss it briefly with the learner. If the learner has trouble completing a plan, the teacher should help by raising the same questions used for C.A.R.E. time: "What do you want?" and "Is what you are doing helping you get what you want?"

When a learner disrupts classroom activities while in the time-out area or fails to follow the plan developed in time-out, he or she may need to take time-out outside the classroom. If possible, the teacher should first discuss behavioral choices with the learner and

---

In-Class Time-Out Form

S.T.A.R. Plan (Success Through Acting Responsibly)

My behavior (What am I doing?)

_____

_____

_____

_____

My plan (I will . . .)

_____

_____

_____

_____

Name _____   Date _____

---

ask if he or she is choosing time-out outside the classroom. If the unacceptable behavior still does not cease, the learner should be sent to the out-of-class time-out area.

The out-of-class time-out area is supervised by an adult who will encourage the learner to discuss what is happening that resulted in a time-out and assist the learner in devising an alternative to the problem behavior in order to return to the classroom as soon as possible. The duration of time-out will vary for each learner. There is no benefit in holding a learner for a set length of time. Such a practice tends to breed resentment, anger, and a desire for revenge. The learner should be allowed to rejoin the class when he or she has developed a satisfactory plan.

In most schools there is a schoolwide time-out room, although it is probably not labeled as such. A learner who exhibits unacceptable behavior is usually referred to the principal's office and engaged either by the principal or another staff member designated to handle discipline problems. This system can rather easily be adapted to the time-out practices described here. It is recommended that the learner have an acceptable written plan before returning to class. A planning sheet similar to the in-class time-out form can be used, and the time-out supervisor can help the learner develop the plan and complete the form. A conference with the classroom teacher is also called for, not to punish the learner but to ensure that the plan has been thought through and that the learner has evaluated the previous behavior. This conference also reestablishes the teacher's and the learner's shared responsibility to preserve the learning environment and to strive for quality.

Classroom interventions generally are triggered in one of two circumstances: when the learner does not do what he or she needs to do to support the community or when the learner needs to make a plan to help him or her get what he or she needs. The normal classroom strategies are employed until the learner's responses are clearly defiant or the lack of response is clearly intended. Classroom interventions with defiant or unresponsive learners are somewhat different from the interventions with those learners who are simply choosing inappropriate behavior and when asked to self-evaluate, display a willingness to do so in good faith. Whereas normal classroom strategies involve directing a number of questions toward the learner, statements made directly and persistently are likely more appropriate for unresponsive/defiant students. Table 6.2 shows the differences.

Table 6.2
Normal Classroom Strategies versus Responses with Unresponsive/Defiant Students

Normal classroom strategies	With unresponsive/defiant students
Ask reality therapy questions.	*Turn the question into a statement.*
What do you want?	This is what I need from you.
What is our rule?	I need you to follow our rule _____.
What are you doing? Saying?	This is what I see. Hear.
Is it working for you?	It's not working for me/us.
Is it following the rule?	Our rule is _____.
Can you figure out a better way?	This is what I want you to (be able to) do.

The sample interchanges between teacher and defiant/unresponsive student included in Table 6.3 illustrate the form actual dialogue might take.

Table 6.3

Sample Interchanges between Teacher and Unresponsive/Defiant Student

---

Dialogue 1

What's the rule? What's our rule about _____?

"I don't know."

The rule is _____.

"I don't care."

Can you do it anyway?

Silence plus nonverbal compliance

Thank you, I appreciate it. (Don't hover; move on.)

Dialogue 2

What are you doing?

Silence or "Nothing" or "What's it to you?"

What I see/hear you doing is _____.

Silence or "So?"

Is it working for you?

"Yes."

I understand . . . but it is not working for us. We need a better plan.

(Wait for student to answer.)

(If no answer) What is your plan?

"I don't have one."

Could you choose to _____?

Dialogue 3

Student is upset.

What do you want/need?

Why is it important to you?

How will it be better if you get what you want?

What does it mean to you?

Dialogue 4

Student complains; blames others.

How would you like it to be?

What do you want to be seeing? Hearing?

What do you think is a solution?

Dialogue 5

Student cries, whines, argues, says, "Everyone is doing it."

That behavior won't work!

This is how you get what you want from me: Ask me.

or Tell me what you need.

The following three exchanges—between a time-out supervisor and a learner, an assistant principal and a learner, and a student dean and a learner—illustrate the use of reality therapy to help these learners plan for different behavior:

TIME-OUT SCENARIO 1

Supervisor: *Sam, I understand there was a problem in class. Let's see if we can work it out.[6]*

Sam: *Nobody ever listens to me.*

Supervisor: *I'll listen. Tell me what you were doing in class.*

Sam: *What do you mean?*

Supervisor: *What were you doing when you got sent from the classroom?*

Sam: *Allyn and Stefonce were teasing me about my haircut, and they made me mad. Mrs. Banks sent me here, and it's not my fault.*

Supervisor: *Allyn and Stefonce were making fun of your haircut, and you're mad at them. What did you do while they were teasing you?*

Sam: *I yelled at them. Mrs. Banks asked me if I was choosing time-out when I started yelling. They didn't stop laughing when she said that, so I just kept on yelling. She wouldn't listen to me. She said I was disrupting the class. It's not my fault.*

Supervisor:	*Do you have a right to be happy and to be treated with compassion in the classroom?*
Sam:	*Yes.*
Supervisor:	*What's the responsibility that goes with that right?*
Sam:	*Not to tease others or hurt anyone's feelings. But I wasn't the one doing the teasing.*
Supervisor:	*Do you have a right to hear and be heard in the classroom?*
Sam:	*Yes. But Mrs. Banks wouldn't listen to me.*
Supervisor:	*What is the responsibility that goes with the right to hear and be heard?*
Sam:	*Not to yell or scream or disturb others.*
Supervisor:	*What were you doing?*
Sam:	*Yelling.*
Supervisor:	*What do you want?*
Sam:	*I want Mrs. Banks to make Stefonce and Allyn stop making fun of my hair.*
Supervisor:	*You want Allyn and Stefonce to stop teasing you. Was it the teasing that got you in trouble, or was it what you chose to do when they teased you that got you in trouble?*
Sam:	*They made me mad.*
Supervisor:	*What did you choose to do when you got mad?*
Sam:	*I yelled at them.*
Supervisor:	*Did choosing to yell make them stop teasing you?*
Sam:	*No, they just laughed and kept on teasing me.*
Supervisor:	*What do you want?*
Sam:	*I don't want this stupid haircut.*
Supervisor:	*So, you think your haircut is a problem. Can you and I do anything about the haircut?*
Sam:	*I guess not.*
Supervisor:	*What do you really want?*
Sam:	*I want to be in class with my friends, but I don't want to be teased about my hair.*

Supervisor: *You want to be in class with your friends. You don't want to be teased about your hair. Is yelling helping you get what you want?*

Sam: *No.*

Supervisor: *What will help you get what you want?*

Sam: *I don't know.*

Supervisor: *Will yelling help you stay in class with your friends?*

Sam: *No.*

Supervisor: *What might help?*

Sam: *I don't know. Maybe not yelling?*

Supervisor: *Is that something you could do?*

Sam: *I guess so.*

Supervisor: *Do you want to be friends with Allyn and Stefonce?*

Sam: *Yeah, if they stop teasing me.*

Supervisor: *If they tease you again, is there something other than yelling that you could choose to do?*

Sam: *Maybe I could walk away and talk to Mrs. Banks.*

Supervisor: *Could you do that?*

Sam: *Yeah.*

Supervisor: *If you walked away and talked to Mrs. Banks, there are some different things she could do to help you solve the problem.*

Sam: *Like what?*

Supervisor: *She could call a class meeting and discuss the right to be happy and treated with compassion by others in the classroom and the responsibility to treat others with compassion. She could refer the three of you to mediation so you could work out your problem face-to-face without disrupting the classroom. Do either of these sound like plans that could help in the future?*

Sam: *Yes, I think so.*

Supervisor: *There is also something else that you might do instead of yelling.*

Sam: There is? I can't think of anything.

Supervisor: Could you tell Allyn and Stefonce how you feel? Maybe say, "I want you to stop teasing. It hurts my feelings." You might even remind them of the Rights and Responsibilities.

Sam: What if that doesn't work? I think they would laugh at me if I said that to them.

Supervisor: What do you want your plan to be?

Sam: I will not yell and disrupt the class. I will ask for Mrs. Banks to help when I get mad.

Supervisor: Do you think this plan will work?

Sam: Well, I won't get sent out of class.

Supervisor: Will you do it?

Sam: Yes.

Supervisor: Will you talk to Allyn and Stefonce?

Sam: Maybe. I'll think about it.

Supervisor: If you want to talk about that, I'll listen. I think you're ready to return to class. Are you? What are you going to say to Mrs. Banks?

Sam: I'll say, "I'm not going to yell in class anymore. If I have a problem, I'm going to ask you to help me."

TIME-OUT SCENARIO 2

Assistant Principal: What happened in class?

Brian: Jason brought a Game Boy to class and was playing with it in his desk. We were all looking at it when Ms. Miller asked me to pay attention.

Assistant Principal: You were watching Jason play a video game in class, and Ms. Miller sent you here.

Brian: Not exactly.

Assistant Principal: Then what, exactly?

Brian: Well, after she got on me, Jason began to laugh. I got mad because she was

	blaming me for something Jason was doing, and Jason was laughing at me. So I yelled at him. Then Ms. Miller asked me if I needed to take a time-out. I guess I yelled at her that Jason should be sent to time-out.
Assistant Principal:	*You were upset because Ms. Miller blamed you alone for disrupting the class and also because Jason was laughing at you. Did you act responsibly when that happened?*
Brian:	*What do you mean?*
Assistant Principal:	*Do you have the right to hear and be heard in this school?*
Brian:	*Yeah, that's on the Rights and Responsibilities poster.*
Assistant Principal:	*What is the responsibility that corresponds to that right?*
Brian:	*I guess it means that I will help keep a calm and quiet school by not yelling or disturbing others.*
Assistant Principal:	*What did you do in class?*
Brian:	*I yelled at Jason for laughing at me. Ms. Miller probably thinks I yelled at her too, but I was just upset.*
Assistant Principal:	*What did you want to accomplish when you were yelling?*
Brian:	*I wanted Jason to stop making fun of me for getting in trouble.*
Assistant Principal:	*You want Jason to stop making fun of you. Was it Jason's behavior or your behavior that got you sent here?*
Brian:	*Well, Jason was playing the game, and I got in trouble for just looking at him.*
Assistant Principal:	*Yes, you've told me that already. But did Ms. Miller send you here after she*

	asked you to pay attention to the les-son?
Brian:	*What do you mean?*
Assistant Principal:	*Did Ms. Miller tell you to leave the class because you were watching Jason and not paying attention?*
Brian:	*No, I guess not. She asked for the time-out after I started yelling at Jason.*
Assistant Principal:	*Would it be accurate to say you got into trouble because you yelled at Jason?*
Brian:	*But I just wanted him to stop laughing.*
Assistant Principal:	*OK, you yelled because you wanted Jason to stop laughing at you. What got you into trouble?*
Brian:	*Yelling.*
Assistant Principal:	*What do you really want?*
Brian:	*I want to get through class without being laughed at for something I didn't do.*
Assistant Principal:	*You want to study without being made fun of for things you didn't do. Did yelling get you this?*
Brian:	*No.*
Assistant Principal:	*What could help you get this?*
Brian:	*I could do what the teacher asks me to do and talk to Jason calmly about the way he treated me. After class might be a good time to talk to Jason.*
Assistant Principal:	*How would that help?*
Brian:	*I probably wouldn't get in trouble with Ms. Miller, and I might be more calm when I tell Jason how I felt.*
Assistant Principal:	*OK! That sounds like a better plan. What else could you do?*
Brian:	*I could also explain everything to Ms. Miller.*

Assistant Principal:	*How and when?*
Brian:	*Probably when she finishes the lesson, maybe after class, and also calmly.*
Assistant Principal:	*Do you expect Ms. Miller to do something? What can Ms. Miller do that would help you?*
Brian:	*She might talk to Jason about how he treated me. She could also sit down with both of us to talk about what happened.*
Assistant Principal:	*She might also talk with the whole class about the right to hear and be heard and the corresponding responsibility to not yell or disturb others. How does that sound?*
Brian:	*I don't know if I want the entire class to talk about how I acted in class.*
Assistant Principal:	*OK. So what would you like to do?*
Brian:	*I will talk to Jason after class today and also explain myself to Ms. Miller.*
Assistant Principal:	*Do you think you can do it?*
Brian:	*I think I can.*
Assistant Principal:	*What if Ms. Miller chooses not to do anything more? What if she doesn't talk to Jason?*
Brian:	*I need to work stuff out with Jason. I guess it's really not Ms. Miller's problem.*
Assistant Principal:	*So, do you have a workable plan? When will you do it?*
Brian:	*Today, as soon as I can talk to Ms. Miller. I'll talk to Jason today, too.*
Assistant Principal:	*Thanks, Brian. If you need any help with this, I'll be willing. Here's a pass. You may return to your regular schedule.*

TIME-OUT SCENARIO 3

Dean: *Jessica, what happened in class? Why are you in time-out?*

Jessica: *I was getting my pencil back from Staci, and she called me a name. I pushed her after she called me the name and Mr. Aleota told me to take a time-out.*

Dean: *You were trying to get the pencil you loaned to Staci. You were upset because she called you a name, so you pushed her.*

Jessica: *I didn't loan her the pencil; she took it. That's why I was upset, and that's why this all happened.*

Dean: *Do you think you should not be in time-out?*

Jessica: *Yeah! This is all Staci's fault.*

Dean: *Do you have the right to be safe in the school?*

Jessica: *Yes. That's on the Rights and Responsibilities.*

Dean: *OK! What's the responsibility that goes with the right to be safe?*

Jessica: *I can't hit or push anyone. But I also have the right to expect my property to be safe in the school.*

Dean: *That's correct, the Rights and Responsibilities refer to persons and to property. Can we look at this further? Do you think it is your right to hit someone because the person took your property?*

Jessica: *Probably not.*

Dean: *Probably?*

Jessica: *No, I don't have the right to hit anyone. OK?*

Dean: *So what is the responsibility that corresponds to your right to expect your property to be safe?*

Jessica: *Staci will not take my property without my permission.*

Dean: *That's Staci's responsibility. What is yours?*

Jessica: *What do you mean?*

Dean: *Look at the Rights and Responsibilities poster. What is your responsibility for your property?*

Jessica: *To keep my property secure.*

Dean: *OK, now what happened in class?*

Jessica: *Staci wouldn't give my pencil back, and she called me a name, so I pushed her.*

Dean: *What did you want Staci to do?*

Jessica: *To give my pencil back and stop calling me names.*

Dean: *You want Staci to return your pencil and stop calling you names. Was it Staci's behavior or your own that was the reason Mr. Aleota sent you here for time-out?*

Jessica: *She got me in trouble by taking my pencil.*

Dean: *Did Mr. Aleota send you here because Staci took your pencil?*

Jessica: *Not really. He sent me to time-out after I pushed Staci.*

Dean: *You were sent here because you pushed Staci. You say you pushed her because you wanted her to return your pencil and stop calling you names. What do you really want?*

Jessica: *I told you, I want my pencil back.*

Dean: *Why is the pencil so important?*

Jessica: *It's my only one, and I can't get any work done without a pencil.*

Dean: *Do you want to get your school work done?*

Jessica: *What I want is for other people to return my things and not call me names so I can do my work.*

Dean: *You want not to have to worry about your property so you can focus on your school work. Did pushing Stacy help you with your school work? Did it make her return your pencil or stop calling you names?*

Jessica: *No.*

Dean: *What can help you get your pencil while not being called names?*

Jessica: *I could tell Mr. Aleota that Staci took my pencil so that he can get it back for me.*

Dean: *Could you do anything else?*

Jessica: *I suppose I could explain to Staci that I think she has my pencil instead of yelling at her and then pushing her.*

Dean: *Oh, you yelled at Staci.*

Jessica: *Yeah, that's why she called me a fat, big-mouthed turd.*

Dean: *So you think you might ask Staci if that could be your pencil she is using. What if she says it is not your pencil?*

Jessica: *I don't know. I guess I could ask someone if I could borrow a pencil.*

Dean: *Great. What else can you do?*

Jessica: *I can ask Mr. Aleota to have a class talk about the right to have property safe in the school.*

Dean: *I suppose he might also talk about each student's right to be safe in the school—safe from being accused and safe from being pushed. Does that sound good?*

Jessica: *Maybe.*

Dean: *You have some good ideas. Which ones would you like to try?*

Jessica: *I don't want to talk alone with Staci right now, so I'll ask Mr. Aleota to talk to her and me. I don't think I want Mr. Aleota to have a class meeting about the right to be safe in the school. I think that too many people would think they were talking about Staci and me. Maybe this would work later. I will borrow a pencil from someone and get to work.*

Dean: *Do you think you can do those things?*

Jessica: *I can. Can I borrow a pencil?*

Dean: *Sure. Will you do me a favor?*

Jessica: *What?*

Dean: *Will you explain your plan to Mr. Aleota when he has time to talk with you?*

Jessica: *OK! Can I go back to class?*

Guidelines for C.A.R.E. Time and Time-Out

Plans developed in C.A.R.E. time or in time-out should meet the following criteria:

- Simple: The plan should be understandable and attainable.

- Specific: The plan should clearly specify the behavior, when and where it is to be exhibited, etc.

- Personal: The plan is for the individual and is as much as possible independent of the actions of others.

- Positive: The plan is an action tied to basic need satisfaction.

- Immediate: The plan should be something that is implemented within the day.

The classroom climate established is an extremely important factor in assisting learners to grow in emotional intelligence and develop a repertoire of responsible behaviors. Learners need a friendly, supportive atmosphere to engage productively in self-evaluation and to risk trying new behaviors. A relationship of mutual appreciation and trust between the teacher and each learner is required for the maximum development of community in which each can fully develop citizenship skills. This relationship depends heavily on a system of rules and expectations that is sensible and predictable. The success of each person in achieving quality depends above all else on the absence of coercion on the part of learner or teacher. The teacher's most important challenge in the classroom to promote the development of emotional intelligence is to relate consistently in a noncoercive way to each learner. Unfortunately, much of what teachers have personally experienced and most of the behavior management practices in existence are coercive. For the most part, there are not good models out there from which to draw. This approach requires us—the adults in the schools—to both redesign our system and learn new behaviors. Neither requirement is easy to achieve. With effort, persistence, vision, and support, we adults can learn to operate in this way—we must for the sake of our future.

Endnotes

1. W. Glasser, *Schools without Failure* (New York: Harper and Row, 1969), 124.

2. D. K. Crawford, R. J. Bodine, and R. G. Hoglund, *The School for Quality Learning: Managing the School and Classroom the Deming Way* (Champaign, IL: Research Press, 1993), 190–191.

3. R. J. Bodine, D. K. Crawford, and F. Schrumpf, *Creating the Peaceable School: A Comprehensive Program for Teaching Conflict Resolution* (Champaign, IL: Research Press, 1994), 29–30.

4. Crawford et al., *The School for Quality Learning.*

5. Crawford et al., *The School for Quality Learning,* 195–196.

6. Crawford et al., *The School for Quality Learning,* 202–203.

CHAPTER 7

Extending Emotional Intelligence through Conflict Resolution Education

Conflict resolution education is an integral part of the program to develop emotional intelligence. A program of conflict resolution education is a program of action strategies that utilizes the four principles of conflict resolution to plan future behaviors. A conflict resolution education program in the schools deals with behavior in its totality by emphasizing planning to act (doing) and affording sufficient practice in both planning and trying out those plans. Because much of what is perceived in schools as misbehavior is unresolved conflict and because the essence of conflict resolution is planning alternate future behaviors, a noncoercive behavior management plan would be incomplete without an educational component that enables learners to resolve conflicts constructively, both with and without adult assistance.

An authentic conflict resolution education program consists of three components: (a) a set of problem-solving principles, (b) a structured process, and (c) the skills for creative cooperation between individuals and among groups.[1] Underlying a conflict resolution education program are certain precepts:

- Conflict is natural and normal.

- Differences can be acknowledged and appreciated.

- Conflict, when viewed as a solution-building opportunity, can lead to positive change.

- When the conflicting parties build on one another's strengths to find solutions, a climate is created that nurtures individual self-worth and opportunities for fulfillment of each individual's needs.

Peace is essential to human survival—individually and collectively—inherent in human development, and originates within each of us. Peace is most often regarded as an outcome or a goal instead of as a behavior. When peace is viewed as an outcome or goal, the emphasis is usually that of reducing war or violence. The problem with this perspective is that peace becomes the end and not the means of preventing war or violence. Viewing peace as an outcome or goal has an effect similar to holding negative perceptions about conflict. Such a view hinders the pursuit of effective behaviors toward resolving disputes before violence ensues. When peace is perceived as more than a state of existence, emphasis shifts toward the behavior of peacemaking. Peace will not become a way of life if it is perceived as an end state. Peace is not static. Peace is dynamic, a present and future behavior, originated and sustained by individuals acting as peacemakers. Peacemaking is behaving in harmony with a larger whole, a harmony that begins within each individual and is connected to and part of a social integrity that sanctions one to live without violating the human rights of others.

From this view, peacemaking obviously fits into the social context of the school pursuing the development of emotional intelligence through classroom management. Conflict resolution education equips individuals to act as peacemakers; peacemakers are emotionally intelligent individuals. The social system and the individuals within that system operationalize the notion that peace is that state where, in any specific context, each individual fully exercises his or her responsibilities to ensure that all individuals fully enjoy all the rights accorded to any one individual in that context. Peace is that state when every individual is able to survive and thrive without being hampered by conflict, prejudice, hatred, antagonism, or injustice. Is the goal of creating a sense of community in schools not actually the goal of creating peace?

Perceptions of Peace

Perceptions of peace are diverse. Positive interpretations of peace tend to evoke abstract rather than concrete images—serenity, calm, contentment—and are articulated more as inspiration than as practice. Peace is often viewed, especially by youth, as something that is weak, passive, dull, or boring. It is little wonder that most people do not perceive peace as something that they make because peace is not first understood as something concrete or practical. People who make peace perceive it simply as the practice of honoring self, one another, and the environment. Peacemakers view themselves as responsible for the health, survival, and integrity of the world, whether that world be the classroom, school, community, or earth. Thus, peacemakers are by definition responsible citizens.

Peacemaking Behavior

Peace is a total behavior and is made day by day, moment by moment, within each of us and by each of us. The behavior of peace might be best understood by contrasting the components of total peacemaker behavior with those of total peacebreaker behavior (see Table 7.1).

Table 7.1
Peacemaker versus Peacebreaker Behaviors

	Peacemaker	Peacebreaker
Doing	risking	reserving
	expanding	withdrawing
	persuading	forcing
	communicating	coercing
	inventing	diminishing
	supporting	punishing
Thinking	concerning	repulsing
	creating	positioning
	imagining	blocking
	respecting	rejecting
	reflecting	blaming
Feeling	caring	hating
	calming	angering
	stimulating	fearing
	harmonizing	frustrating

Peacemakers usually honor themselves and others, pursue fairness and justice without violence, protect and promote human rights, and maintain fulfilling human relationships. They have a success identity. Peacebreakers usually do not honor themselves and others, do not pursue fairness and justice without violence nor protect and promote human rights, and do not maintain fulfilling human relationships. They have a failure identity.

To peacebreakers, the notion of justice is at best compensatory and at worst retaliatory. Peacebreakers seek retribution from those who threaten or harm them. They react negatively and often aggressively toward those who challenge their notion of what is "right" or "should be," even when those with other points of view express those views in nonthreatening, reasonable ways. Peacebreakers see limited potential in others and in relationships. Peacebreakers hold themselves in reserve from others, from their own problems, and from their behavioral alternatives. Peacebreakers do not own problems; problems are someone else's fault, and someone else is responsible for solving them. Peacebreakers see themselves as disconnected from the world and its people. Peacebreakers are lacking in emotional intelligence. These individuals either do not understand how to behave or choose not to behave as peacemakers, likely because they lack understanding of their basic needs or see few options for gaining need satisfaction.

On the other hand, peacemakers perceive themselves as connected to the world and its people. Peacemakers are reflective thinkers and listeners, who understand personal, social, and global realities. Peacemakers see themselves as responsible for finding solutions to problems and taking risks to create new possibilities. Peacemakers even attempt, to the best of their ability, to reconcile conflicts within themselves—they strive to balance their needs. Peacemakers possess emotional intelligence.

Constructive conflict resolution is peacemaking. Animosity and violence occur because conflict resolution methods have not been learned or are not practiced. Adults and children can incorporate peacemaking into their daily lives by learning and practicing the principles of conflict resolution.

Practices for Managing Conflict in Schools

Conflict resolution differs from common approaches toward solving problems, especially in schools. Teachers, administrators, and other staff charged with managing student behavior in schools are all too aware of interpersonal and intergroup conflict. A considerable component of these adults' responsibilities within the school community is managing conflict. Schools do manage behavior arising from conflict, but it is clear that these methodologies should be rethought.

There are many possibilities for problem solving between people or groups of people. One problem-solving strategy, arbitration, is the process whereby a party not involved directly in the conflict determines a solution to the conflict; the arbitrator rules, and the disputants are expected to comply with the ruling.

Schools rely almost exclusively on arbitration, with the adult authority serving as arbitrator to settle the dispute for the parties, whereas conflict resolution involves bringing the parties of the dispute together, providing them the processes to resolve the dispute and expecting them to do so. Students often perceive the process of arbitration as coercive—someone else is "telling us what to do." This is true even when they recognize that the directive may be in their best interests. The problem-solving strategies of conflict resolution are future directed: The disputants craft and commit to a plan of action to behave differently from this point forward.[2] These strategies are noncoercive, planning tools for responsible behavior.

Clearly, the strategies of a conflict resolution education program differ from the prevalent practices for managing student conflict. Conflict resolution consists of cooperative, collaborative problem-solving methodologies in which those with ownership of the problem participate directly in crafting a solution to the problem, with or without involvement of others. Table 7.2 details the differences between prevalent practices and conflict resolution strategies.

Table 7.2
Prevalent Practices versus Conflict Resolution

Prevalent practices	Conflict resolution
Relies on a third party to settle disputes	Directly involves the conflicting parties in both resolution process and outcome
Reactively offers services after the conflict occurs	Proactively offers skills and strategies to participants prior to their involvement in the conflict
Focuses on conflict after a school rule has been broken; often advice is to ignore problem if it is thought to not be major or serious	Intervenes in conflicts and prevents their escalation into the broken-rule stage or into violence
Uses arbitration almost exclusively to settle disputes	Maximizes the use of negotiation and mediation processes to resolve disputes
Requires adults to spend a disproportionate amount of time dealing with minor student conflicts	Uses teacher and virtually unlimited student resources to handle such conflicts and learn essential decision-making skills in the process
Relies on disciplinary codes that are ineffective at helping students reconcile interpersonal and intergroup differences	Focuses attention not on the disciplinary offense but on how to resolve the interpersonal and intergroup dimensions of a conflict

Conflict Resolution

Not all disputes may be settled by students, using the problem-solving strategies of conflict resolution. There are instances where an adult may need to be involved in the conflict resolution process. There are other instances where the adult authority may determine that the obvious issue of the dispute (e.g., a fight between two students) is not appropriate for mediation or negotiation, even though the long-term relationship issues of the dispute might be suitable for cooperative, collaborative problem solving. Cases also exist in which the disputants will choose, for any number of reasons, not to participate in the problem-solving process. In any of these scenarios, arbitration in some form is likely the most practical alternative available. The proposed behavior management program may not eliminate the use of arbitration as a problem-solving strategy, but it will reduce reliance on it as a management process.

The problem-solving strategies of conflict resolution are consensual: The disputants must agree to participate in any of the cooperative, collaborative processes and to work toward resolution. According to Fisher, Ury, and Patton, the BATNA, or the best alternative to a negotiated agreement, is a prime determinant in whether one participates in the problem-solving strategies of conflict resolution.[3] The reason one negotiates is to produce something better than the result one could obtain without negotiating. A person will likely choose not to participate in consensual problem solving if he or she believes doing so might be detrimental to satisfaction of his or her needs—in other words, if the individual's belief is that the BATNA will be superior to a negotiated outcome. A person volunteers to participate in the belief that doing so will enhance the opportunity to satisfy his or her needs—that is, if any of the perceived outcomes seems superior to his or her BATNA. The question "What might happen if you don't reach an agreement?" is useful in assessing the BATNA.

The BATNA is actually an individual's perception of the potential outcomes of problem solving. An educational goal for conflict resolution education is to help people assess their BATNAs creatively and accurately, to bring these perceptions closer to reality. An accurate BATNA protects people from accepting agreements that are unfavorable and from rejecting agreements that would be in their long-term best interests. Becoming proficient in the principles of conflict resolution enables people to base assessment of their BATNAs on understanding rather than fear and to approach situations with an "abundance mentality" rather than a "scarcity mentality." When this happens, people are more likely to choose to be directly involved in resolving problems that affect them. They will understand that their interests are more likely to be addressed when they inform others of and advocate for those interests. When one learns to self-evaluate to determine the potential of any behavior to provide need satisfaction, one is likely to assess one's BATNA more accurately. Learning to uncover the true origin of a conflict—the fact that individuals employ different methods to satisfy the basic psychological needs of belonging, power, freedom, and fun—is vital to the evaluation.

The following situation illustrates how the BATNA is involved in choosing whether or not to problem solve: Sam and Terry have been friends for several years.[4] In the hallway just before school starts, Terry accuses Sam of spreading rumors about Terry and another student. A loud argument ensues, and Sam shoves Terry into the lockers. At that very moment, a hall supervisor comes around the corner and witnesses the shove. The supervisor sends Sam to the dean's office. The dean assigns Sam to in-school suspension and also suggests that Sam and Terry request a mediation to try to work out their problem. Sam has no choice but to serve the suspension. The decision whether to mediate (negotiate an agreement) will be a shared choice depending upon Sam's BATNA and Terry's BATNA: What is the best they can expect if they do not deal directly with each other? Sam's BATNA is that Terry will likely continue to think Sam is spreading rumors and will remain angry at Sam for the shoving incident. Their friendship will be damaged. Terry's BATNA is that Sam will likely be mad at Terry and blame Terry for causing the argument that resulted in Sam's suspension. Their friendship will be damaged. If the mutual friendship is important to Sam and Terry, their BATNAs would suggest that a negotiated agreement is advisable since their best alternative to doing so is very likely a damaged relationship. Through negotiation or mediation, they can develop options to address relationship concerns—such as confidentiality and trust—and thus can continue as friends. If the friendship is not important to one or both of them, or if they believe they can continue to coexist in the school without future problems, they will have little motivation to negotiate or mediate an agreement.

Perceptions of Conflict

If we accept that much of what is termed misbehavior in schools is rooted in conflict, an in-depth understanding of conflict is necessary to help students learn to deal with it constructively.

Without conflict, there would likely be no personal growth or social change. Unfortunately, when it comes to conflict the perceptions of most people are profoundly negative. When asked to list words or phrases associated with conflict, most adults as well as most children respond negatively: "fight," "hit," "argument," "it's harmful," "yelling," "war," "hate," "get even," and so forth. These negative attitudes about conflict are likely the result of assimilated messages from the media, parents, teachers, friends, government officials, and most others with whom one encounters conflict.

Negative perceptions and the reactions they provoke are extremely detrimental to successful conflict resolution. However, before they can be replaced, they first must be understood. To start, think about your own attitudes toward conflict: Does denying the existence of conflict help you resolve it? Does accusing or defending help you to cooperate? Can you make a conflict go away by not thinking about it? Are you really able to force another person to change? Does assuming there will be a winner and a loser help?

In every conflict, each individual has a choice—to be driven by these negative perceptions or to take control of the situation and act in a positive way. With more personal awareness and better understanding of available choices, one becomes able to approach conflict knowing that it can have either destructive or constructive results. When conflict is perceived as a positive life force, those in conflict become responsible for producing a result in which relationships are enhanced and individuals are empowered to control their own lives in ways that respect the needs of others. The power to create resolution lies within each person. However, perhaps largely because of the absence of observable models, this power is most often not utilized. The purpose of a behavior management program that embraces conflict resolution education is to provide students and adults with the knowledge and skills to unleash this power.

It is important to realize that students' success in developing awareness of the positive potential of conflict is an outgrowth of the endeavors and commitment exhibited by the adults in the school to approach conflict in a positive way. Teachers who integrate positive ways of resolving conflicts into their classrooms and schools will see results that have a powerful effect on their own lives and work, as well as on the lives and work of their students. These adults will provide powerful behavioral models for their students—not only will they be using conflict resolution processes, they will be doing so in full view of their students. Is this not an overwhelming rationale for the adults in school to abandon coercive management tactics? Who better to serve as positive conflict role models than school personnel?

Origins of Conflict

Diagnosing the origins or sources of a conflict can help define a problem, and a definition of the problem is the starting point in any attempt to find a solution. As discussed in chapter 4, almost every conflict involves an endeavor by the disputants to meet the basic psychological needs for belonging, power, freedom, and fun. Limited resources and different values may appear to be the cause of conflicts, but unmet needs are truly at their root. Conflict resolution is next to impossible as long as one side believes its psychological needs are being threatened by the other. Unless unmet needs are expressed, the conflict will often reappear, even when a solution is reached regarding the subject of the dispute.

Limited resources

Conflicts involving limited resources (time, money, property) typically are the easiest to resolve. People quickly learn that cooperating instead of competing for scarce resources is in their best interests. In cooperation, disputants share in problem solving, recognize each other's interests, and create choices. This process usually provides satisfaction because the psychological needs of belonging and power, perhaps even of freedom and fun, are addressed in the equitable allocation of limited resources. It is important to realize how conflicts over unmet psychological needs are played out against the backdrop of limited resources. For instance, the student who is upset over the fact that his friend has not repaid a loan may really want to know his friend respects him (a power need). He may not easily accept a payment solution unless his need for recognition is addressed in the process. Limited resource conflicts may not be resolved because the resource itself may not define the problem. When solutions are crafted that deal only with the limited resource that seems to be the source of the conflict, the real problem is not solved, and the conflict will return.

Different values

Conflicts involving different values (beliefs, priorities, principles) tend to be more difficult to resolve. When a person holds a value, he or she has an enduring belief that a specific action or quality is preferable to an opposite action or quality. This belief applies to attitudes toward objects, situations, or individuals. The belief becomes a standard that guides the person's actions.

When the terminology used to express a conflict includes words such as *honest, equal, right,* and *fair,* the conflict is typically one of values. Many times disputants think in terms of "right/wrong" or "good/bad" when values are in opposition. Even conflicts over differing goals can be viewed as values conflicts: The source of a goal conflict relates either to the goal's relative importance to each disputant or to the fact that the disputants highly value different goals.

When values are in conflict, the disputants often perceive the dispute as a personal attack or as a serious conflict between a trusted family belief and an alternative way of viewing the issue. They tend to personalize the conflict because they feel their whole sense of self is threatened and under attack. Strong stances on principle are therefore characteristic of value conflicts. When people feel attacked, they typically become defensive and cling stubbornly to their own convictions. The conflict exists because the disputants are governed by different sets of rules. Because the disputants evaluate the problem and each other according to conflicting criteria, resolution can be especially difficult.

Values disputes, rooted in issues of social diversity (differences in cultural, social, and physical/mental attributes, and religious affiliations), are often expressed as different beliefs, convictions, and/or principles, but they also often involve prejudice. Although complex, such conflicts can be resolved by increased awareness, understanding, and tolerance. When a conflict is rooted in prejudice or bias against a fellow student—as a member of a group perceived as inferior, strange, even dangerous—ignorance, fear, and misunderstanding often guide behavior toward that person. Also, an unexamined sense of status or privilege may inadvertently hurt the other disputant through certain behaviors resulting in exclusion, isolation, or lack of recognition. Verbal expressions of this sense of ascendancy or privilege may even constitute racial or sexual harassment.

Rigid value systems can severely restrict one from meeting the need to belong. The more one adheres to any value, the more one's belonging is limited to others who hold the same beliefs and the less exposure one has to diversity. Inflexible values are also almost always destructive to our need to be free. We see others as wrong if they do not hold our beliefs, and we see situations as bad if they do not meet our standards. When this is the case, our options in life to satisfy our needs for freedom, fun, and power—as well as our choice of friends—become limited.

Psychological needs are enmeshed in values conflicts. For example, a person may be in conflict when a friend does not keep a promise. If the person's picture of a friend is that of someone who is reliable, the person's sense of belonging will be threatened because his or her value system includes the assumption that friends do not make promises they cannot keep.

Resolving a values conflict does not mean the disputants must change or align their values. Often a mutual acknowledgment that each person views the situation differently is the first step toward resolution. If the disputants can learn not to reject each other because of differences in beliefs, they will be better able to deal with the problem on its own merits. This is the essence of conflict resolution's attempt to deal separately with relationship and substantive issues. To resolve values conflicts, the disputants must look for interests that underlie the conflicting values. Again, psychological needs are enmeshed in values conflicts, and those needs likely frame the interests of each disputant.

Responses to Conflict

Responses to conflict fall generally into three basic groups: soft responses, hard responses, and principled responses.[5] For both soft and hard responses, participants take positions or stands on the problem. They negotiate these positions by trying either to avoid a contest of will or to win a contest of will. Soft and hard negotiations bring about one-sided losses to reach an agreement or demand one-sided gains as the price of the agreement. For principled responses, participants utilize conflict resolution strategies designed to produce wise agreements. A wise agreement is one that addresses the legitimate interests of both parties, resolves conflicting interests fairly, is durable, and takes contextual interests into account—how others besides the disputants will be affected by the agreement.

Soft responses

Soft responses usually involve people who are friends or people who just want to be nice to each other, probably because it is likely the contact between the parties will continue into the future. In either case, they want to agree, and they negotiate softly to do so. Avoiding conflict is often the first soft response. People attempt to avoid conflict altogether by withdrawing from the situation, ignoring the problem, and denying that the conflict matters. When people choose to avoid conflict, it is usually because they are not interested in maintaining the relationship or because they lack the skills to negotiate a resolution. Accommodation, when one party adjusts to the position of the other without seeking to serve his or her own interests in the relationship, is a common soft response. Soft responses, especially avoidance responses, may have some merit for the immediate situation—for example, they may help a person control anger, protect one from immediate dangers of someone who responds aggressively, or even allow one to buy time to plan a better problem-solving strategy. However, the soft response typically results in feelings of disillusionment, self-doubt, fear, and anxiety about the future. Many compromises are, in reality, soft responses to the conflict. The parties agree to something that addresses only some of each of their needs in order to escape the confrontation.

Hard responses

Hard responses to conflict usually involve people who are adversaries, whose goal is victory. Hard responses to a conflict are characterized by confrontations that involve threats, aggression, and anger. Hard negotiators demand concessions as a condition of the relationship and insist on their position. They often search for a single answer to the problem—the one the other side will give in to. Hard negotiators frequently apply pressure trying to win a contest of will. They use bribery and punishment (e.g., withholding money, favors, and affection). When these intimidating tactics cause the other side to yield, the hard negotiator feels successful. Hostility, physical damage, and violence often result from this type of response to conflict. Furthermore, this attitude is always detrimental to cooperation.

Principled responses

Principled responses involve people who view themselves as problem-solvers, whose goal is a wise outcome reached efficiently and amicably. These problem-solvers have developed communication and conflict resolution skills. Principled negotiators understand that communication is fundamental to cooperative interaction, and they understand what it means to participate in developing a common understanding. Principled responses to conflict are characterized by first seeking to understand the other side, then seeking to be understood. Principled negotiators are skilled, active, empathic listeners. Principled negotiators get inside the other side's frame of reference to see the problem as that person does and to comprehend the person emotionally and intellectually. Principled responses to conflict create the opportunity for each participant to get his or her needs met. Principled responses to conflict are proactive, not reactive. When people behave proactively, they do not feel victimized and out of control—they do not blame other people or circumstances when in conflict. Instead, they take charge of their actions and feelings and utilize their principled negotiation skills to make resolution a possibility.

Outcomes of different responses

The three types of responses to conflict produce different outcomes. Soft responses may be considered a Lose-Lose approach to conflict. When both parties deny the existence of the conflict or when they will deal with only superficial issues and not the interests at the root of the problem, neither person gets what he or she wants—they both lose. In those situations where one side accommodates the other, a Lose-Win situation may result. A person who avoids a conflict by accommodating the other person loses in the sense that he or she has little courage to express personal feelings and convictions and is intimidated by others. When conflicts are avoided, basic psychological needs are not acknowledged or met.

Thus, people who avoid conflicts are not in effective control of their lives; they see themselves as victims, and their relations with others invariably suffer.

Hard responses may be considered a Win-Lose approach to conflict, where the more aggressive individuals win and their adversaries lose. This interpretation of winning and losing is usually in relation to the limited resource involved in the conflict. Often hard responses become Lose-Lose when the desire to punish or get even provokes adversaries to take vindictive actions that harm themselves as well as their opponents. These confrontations often are characterized by the parties each viewing the other as the "enemy" and each being driven to vindictive actions to punish the other or to get even. Hard responses produce stressful situations when the negotiators are required to continue to interact in some manner, perhaps even to continue to work together toward common goals.

Both soft and hard responses are characterized by reactive communication indicating the individual is attempting to transfer responsibility and is not able to choose a response: "There is nothing I can do—I am not responsible."

Principled responses to conflicts change the game and the outcome. Principled methods of conflict resolution produce wise outcomes efficiently and amicably. This response to conflict focuses on interests instead of positions and brings people in conflict to a gradual consensus on a resolution without the transactional costs of digging into positions and without the emotional costs of destroying relationships. Principled responses are characterized by proactive communication indicating the individual takes responsibility for his or her actions and has the ability to choose a response. Principled negotiation is considered a Win-Win response to conflict. Emotionally intelligent people can and do use the principled response frequently in conflict situations.

The challenge in conflict resolution education is to replace commonly held myths about conflict with a view more in line with reality. This, for most, is a major paradigm shift. Table 7.3 exhibits the desired shift in understanding of conflict.

The actions people choose when they are involved in a conflict will either increase or decrease the problem: When conflict escalates, the problem remains unresolved, and the effect can be destructive. As a conflict escalates, threats usually increase and more people become involved and take sides. Anger, fear, and frustration are expressed, sometimes violently. As a conflict escalates, people become more and more entrenched in their positions. Conflicts deescalate when differences and interests are understood. People remain calm and are willing to listen to opposing viewpoints. Those involved focus on the problem rather than on each other and create opportunity for resolution.

Conflict in and of itself is not positive or negative. Rather, the actions chosen turn conflict into a competitive, devastating battle or into a constructive challenge where there is opportunity for growth. One always has the choice, when in conflict, to work for resolution. It is not our choice to be conflict-free—conflict is an inevitable part of life. Our choice is how to deal with those inevitable conflicts. Linking the development of emotional intelligence with an understanding of the potency of conflict resolution equips individuals to be responsible citizens.

The principled approach to conflict is the only way conflicts truly can be resolved. Soft and hard responses only manage conflict—one likely to preserve a relationship, the other designed to

Table 7.3
Conflict Myths and Conflict Realities

Myth	Reality
1. Conflict is always bad.	1. Conflict is neither good nor bad—the behaviors we choose in conflict situations turn conflict into a destructive or constructive force.
2. Conflict is a contest.	2. Many conflicts can be resolved Win-Win; nearly every conflict can be approached Win-Win.
3. There is one right way to approach conflict.	3. There are a variety of ways to respond to a conflict; each different type of response has benefits and limitations.

win the contest. The disadvantage of the principled response to conflict is that it is time consuming. Emotionally intelligent individuals wisely choose the conflicts on which to invest the time needed for resolution.

Principles of Conflict Resolution

The ideas in the book *Getting to Yes*, by Fisher, Ury, and Patton, provide the foundation for teaching students and adults the problem-solving strategies of conflict resolution.[6] The conflict resolution principles—or, in other words, the principled negotiation elements—described in *Getting to Yes* are requisite for any program of conflict resolution. The following discussion illustrates how the four principles in that work are applied in programs to teach conflict resolution strategies.

Separate people from the problem

The first principle, separate people from the problem, concerns people's strong emotions, differing perceptions, and difficulty communicating. When dealing with a problem, it is common for people to misunderstand each other, get upset, and take things personally. Every problem has both substantive issues and relationship issues. Unfortunately, the relationship of the parties tends to become involved in the substance of the problem. Fisher and colleagues assert that "before working on the substantive problem, the 'people problem' should be disentangled from it and dealt with separately. Figuratively, if not literally, the participants should come to see themselves as working side by side, attacking the problem, not each other."[7]

People problems fall into three categories: *perception, emotion,* and *communication.* These problems must be dealt with directly; they cannot be resolved indirectly with substantive concessions. Fisher and colleagues maintain, "Where perceptions are inaccurate, you can look for ways to educate. If emotions run high, you can find ways for each person involved to let off steam. Where misunderstanding exists, you can work to improve communication."[8]

Perception. When dealing with problems of perception, it is important to remember that conflict does not lie in objective reality but in how people perceive the reality. As Fisher, Ury, and Patton point out, "Truth is simply one more argument—perhaps a good one, perhaps not—for dealing with the difference. The difference itself exists because it exists in their thinking. Facts, even if established, may do nothing to solve the problem."[9] Every conflict involves differing points of view; thus, every conflict involves differing notions of what is true, what is false, or the degree to which facts are important. Therefore, the "truth" and its importance are relative.

Emotion. When dealing with problems of emotion, it is important to remember that the parties may be more ready to fight it out than to work together cooperatively to solve the problem. As Fisher and colleagues state, "People often come to a negotiation realizing that the stakes are high and feeling threatened. Emotions on one side will generate emotions on the other. Fear may breed anger; and anger, fear. Emotions may quickly bring a negotiation to an impasse or an end."[10] In conflict resolution the sharing of feelings and emotions is as important as the sharing of perceptions.

Communication. Given the diversity of background and values among individuals, poor communication is not surprising. Conflict resolution strategies are, simply put, processes of communication between disputing parties for the purpose of reaching a joint decision. As Fisher, Ury, and Patton claim, "Communication is never an easy thing even between people who have an enormous background of shared values and experience. . . . It is not surprising, then, to find poor communication between people who do not know each other well and who may feel hostile and suspicious of one another. Whatever you say, you should expect that the other side will almost always hear something different."[11]

There are four basic problems in communication:

1. People may not be talking to each other.

2. Even if they are talking to each other, they may not be hearing each other.

3. What one intends to communicate is almost never exactly what one communicates.

4. People misunderstand or misinterpret that which is communicated.

Techniques for dealing with the problems of perception, emotion, and communication are foundation abilities for conflict resolution. These skills work because the behaviors of separating the relationship from the substantive problem change people from adversaries in a confrontation to partners in a side-by-side search for a fair agreement, advantageous to each.

Focus on interests, not positions

The second principle—focus on interests, not positions—holds that the focus of conflict resolution should not be on the positions held by the people in dispute but on what the people really want— in other words, their interests. The objective of conflict resolution is to satisfy the underlying interests of the parties. Understanding the difference between positions and interests is crucial because interests, not positions, define the problem. Positions are something that people decide they want; interests are what cause people to decide. Fisher and colleagues note that "compromising between positions is not likely to produce an agreement which will effectively take care of the human needs that led people to adopt those positions."[12]

Reconciling interests rather than compromising positions works because for every interest there are usually several possible satisfactory solutions. Furthermore, reconciling interests works because behind opposing positions lie more shared and compatible interests than conflicting ones. Thus, focusing on interests, especially the common and compatible ones, instead of arguing positions, makes it possible to develop solutions. Positions are usually concrete and clearly expressed, often as demands or suggested solutions. But the interests underlying the positions are less tangible and often unexpressed. Asking questions to identify the interests of the parties in a conflict is a foundation ability of conflict resolution.

In almost every conflict, there are multiple interests to consider. Only by talking about and acknowledging interests explicitly can people uncover mutual interests and resolve conflicting interests. In searching for the interests behind people's positions, it is prudent to look particularly for the basic human needs that motivate all people. If basic needs are identified as shared or compatible interests, options can be developed that address these needs. Shared and compatible interests can serve as the building blocks for a wise agreement.

Unless interests are identified, people in conflict will not be able to make wise agreements. A temporary agreement may be reached, but such agreements typically do not last because the real interests have not been addressed. For lasting agreements, interests—not positions—must be the focus. In conflict resolution, each party may not get what he or she wants (the position), but it is possible for each to gain need satisfaction (the interest).

Invent options for mutual gain

The third principle, invent options for mutual gain, allows parties the opportunity to design options that may be potential solutions without the pressure of deciding. Before trying to reach agreement, the parties brainstorm a wide range of possible options that advance shared interests and creatively reconcile differing interests. Fisher, Ury, and Patton say, "In most negotiations there are four major obstacles that inhibit the inventing of an abundance of options: (1) premature judgment; (2) searching for the single answer; (3) the assumptions of a fixed pie; and (4) thinking that 'solving their problem is their problem.' In order to overcome these constraints, you need to understand them."[13]

The problem with premature judgment is that such judgment hinders the process of creating options by limiting imagination. When searching for a single answer, people see their job as narrowing the gap between positions, not broadening the options available. Looking from the outset for the single best answer impedes the wiser decision-making process in which people select from a large number of possible answers. When people make the assumption that resources are finite (i.e., a "fixed pie"), they see the situation as essentially either/or—one person or the other gets what is in dispute. If options are obvious, why bother to invent them? Thinking that solving the problem is the problem presents an obstacle to inventing options because each side's concern is only for its own immediate interests. This shortsighted self-concern leads people to develop only partisan positions, partisan arguments, and one-sided solutions.

The foundation ability of brainstorming is used to separate inventing from deciding. Brainstorming is designed to produce ideas to solve the problem, with the key ground rule being to postpone criticism and evaluation of those ideas. In order to broaden options, those in a dispute should think about the problem in different ways and use ideas to generate other ideas. Inventing options for mutual gain is done by developing possibilities for action that address the shared and compatible interests of the parties in dispute. The final choice of a solution is easier when options that appeal to the interests of both parties exist.

Use objective criteria

The fourth principle, use objective criteria, ensures that the agreement reflects some fair standard instead of the arbitrary will of either side. Using objective criteria means that neither party needs to give in to the other; rather, they can defer to a fair solution. Objective criteria are developed based on fair standards and fair procedures. Objective criteria are independent of will, legitimate, and practical. Theoretically, they can be applied to both sides. In *Getting to Yes,* the authors use the example of the age-old way to divide a piece of cake between two children to illustrate the use of fair standards and procedures: One cuts, and the other chooses. Neither complains about an unfair division. It is important to frame each issue as a joint search for objective criteria, to reason and be open to reason as to which standards are most appropriate and how they should be applied, and to yield only to principle, not pressure of will. Pressure of will can take the form of bribes, threats, manipulative appeals to trust, or simple refusal to budge.

One standard of justification does not exclude the existence of others. When what one side believes to be fair is not what the other believes to be fair, this does not automatically exclude fairness as a criterion or mean that one notion of fairness must be accepted over the other. It does require both parties to explain what that criterion means to them and to respond to reasons for applying another standard or for applying a standard differently. When people advance different standards, the key is to look for an objective basis for deciding between them, such as which standard has been used by the parties in the past or which standard is more widely applied. The principled response is to invite the parties to state their reasoning, to suggest objective criteria, and to operate only on the basis of these principles. Plainly, a refusal to yield accompanied by sound reasons is an easier position to defend—publicly and privately—than is a refusal to yield combined with a refusal to advance sound reasons. One who insists that problem solving be based on merits can bring others around to adopting that tactic once it becomes clear that to do so is the only way to advance substantive interests. The critical thinking abilities of establishing criteria and evaluating possibilities based on criteria are foundation abilities for conflict resolution.

Foundation Abilities for Conflict Resolution

In the problem-solving strategies of conflict resolution, certain attitudes, understandings, and skills are facilitative and/or essential. For problem solving in conflict situations to be effective, attitudes and understandings ultimately must be translated into behaviors— that is, into foundation abilities. Although considerable overlap and interplay exists, these foundation abilities involve the following clusters of behaviors.

Orientation abilities

Orientation abilities encompass the values, beliefs, attitudes, and propensities compatible with effective conflict resolution. They include the following:

- Nonviolence
- Compassion and empathy
- Fairness
- Trust
- Justice
- Tolerance
- Self-respect
- Respect for others
- Celebration of diversity
- Appreciation of controversy

These values, beliefs, attitudes, and propensities can be developed through teaching activities that promote cooperation and prejudice reduction. Orientation abilities culminate in an internalization that every conflict presents an opportunity to learn and grow if one chooses to approach it constructively and creatively.

Perception abilities

Perception abilities encompass the understanding that conflict does not lie in objective reality but in how people perceive that reality. Perception abilities include the following:

- Empathizing in order to see the situation as the other side sees it

- Self-evaluating to recognize personal fears and assumptions

- Suspending judgment and blame to facilitate a free exchange of views

- Reframing solutions to allow for face-saving and to preserve self-respect and self-image

These abilities enable one to develop self-awareness and to assess the limitations of one's own perceptions. They also enable one to work to understand others' points of view. The culminating notion is that differences in point of view exist for many reasons and that labeling points of view in a polarized fashion is not helpful in resolving issues between individuals.

Emotion abilities

Emotion abilities encompass behaviors to manage anger, frustration, fear, and other emotions. These abilities include the following:

- Learning the language of emotions and developing the courage to make emotions explicit

- Expressing emotions in nonaggressive, noninflammatory ways

- Exercising self-control in order to control one's reaction to others' emotional outbursts

These abilities enable one to gain the self-confidence and self-control needed to confront and resolve the conflict. The basis for these behaviors is acknowledging that emotions—often strong ones—are present in conflict, that those emotions may not always be expressed, and that emotional responses by one party may trigger emotional responses from another party. Emotional intelligence is basic to constructive conflict resolution because these abilities strongly influence all the other foundation abilities.

Communication abilities

Communication abilities encompass behaviors of listening and speaking that allow for the effective exchange of facts and feelings. These abilities are as follows:

- Listening to understand
- Speaking to be understood
- Reframing emotionally charged statements into neutral, less emotional terms

These abilities include the skills of active listening, which allows one to (a) attend to another person and that person's message, (b) summarize that message to check out what was heard and advise the other person of the message received, and (c) ask open-ended, nonleading questions to solicit additional information that might clarify the conflict. Also included are the skills of speaking to be understood rather than to debate or impress, speaking about yourself by describing the problem in terms of its impact upon you, speaking with clarity and concision to convey your purpose, and speaking in a style that makes it as easy as possible for the other party to hear. The skill of reframing, coupled with acknowledging strong emotions, is highly useful in conflict resolution. Participatory conflict resolution, in which those who own the conflict work for resolution, is simply a communication process.

Creative thinking abilities

Creative thinking abilities encompass behaviors that enable people to be innovative in problem definition and decision making. These abilities are as follows:

- Contemplating the problem from a variety of perspectives

- Approaching the problem-solving task as a mutual pursuit of possibilities

- Brainstorming to create, elaborate, and enhance a variety of options

Included is the skill of uncovering the interests of the parties involved in a conflict through questioning to identify what the parties want, as well as probing deeper by seeking to understand why they want what they want. The skill of problem definition involves stating the problem, and thus the problem-solving task, as a pursuit of options to satisfy the interests of each party. Flexibility in responding to situations and in accepting a variety of choices and potential solutions is an essential skill in decision making. The behavior is brainstorming—separating the process of generating ideas from the act of judging them. Also critical to success is the ability to elaborate potential solutions and to enhance and embellish existing solutions.

Critical thinking abilities

Critical thinking abilities encompass the behaviors of analyzing, hypothesizing, predicting, strategizing, comparing and contrasting, and evaluating. Included are the following:

- Recognizing and making explicit existing criteria

- Establishing objective criteria

- Applying criteria as the basis for choosing options

- Planning future behaviors

These foundation abilities are integral to the facilitation of the four principles of conflict resolution: separating people from the problem; focusing on interests, not positions; inventing options for mutual gain; and using objective criteria as the basis for decision-making. Thus, they are necessary for the utilization of the problem-solving strategies of conflict resolution. Since most, if not all, are also abilities central to learning in general, they can be developed in schools in a variety of ways; many separate from the issue of personal conflict. Although these abilities are essential for using the problem-solving strategies of conflict resolution, programs that teach these abilities are not always conflict resolution education programs. Conflict resolution involves developing these abilities and then using them to carry out a problem-solving strategy that includes the four principles of conflict resolution. When conflict resolution problem-solving strategies and the abilities necessary to carry out the strategies are learned and practiced, students and adults are better able to resolve their own disputes and assist others in resolving disputes. Those individuals are emotionally intelligent.

Conflict Resolution Problem-Solving Processes

Genuine conflict resolution education programs employ the four principles of conflict resolution through a structured problem-solving process (negotiation, mediation, or consensus decision making) designed to allow the participants to successfully exhibit the behaviors intrinsic to the foundation abilities. The conflict resolution processes are characterized by a series of steps that enable the disputants to identify their own needs and interests and to work cooperatively to find solutions to meet those needs and interests. The structured process gives support and direction to the cooperative effort, assisting the parties to stay focused on the problem and not each other, and to find a mutually acceptable resolution. In addition, genuine conflict resolution education programs include extensive training and practice in using the principles and problem-solving processes of conflict resolution.

The six basic steps in each conflict resolution problem-solving process are:

1. Set the stage
2. Gather perspectives
3. Identify interests
4. Create options
5. Evaluate options
6. Generate agreement

Conflict Resolution Problem-Solving Strategies

The problem-solving strategies of conflict resolution are negotiation, mediation, and consensus decision making. In each strategy, the parties of the dispute work through a cooperative, collaborative procedure that incorporates the four principles of conflict resolution. Through the principles of conflict resolution the procedure enables the parties to maximize the potential that a resolution will be crafted that satisfies the interests of each party. Each of the three conflict resolution strategies is based on negotiation theory, and although the terms, especially negotiation and mediation, may be used interchangeably in conflict resolution literature and practice, here they are defined as follows:

- *Negotiation* is a problem-solving process in which the two parties in the dispute, or representatives of the two parties, meet face to face to work together, unassisted, to resolve the dispute.

- *Mediation* is a problem-solving process in which the two parties in the dispute, or representatives of the two parties, meet face to face to work together, assisted by a neutral third party called the mediator, to resolve the dispute.

- *Consensus decision making* is a group problem solving process in which all of the parties in the dispute, or representatives of each party, meet to collaborate to resolve the dispute by crafting a plan of action that all parties can and will support. This process may or may not be facilitated by a neutral party.

The goal of conflict resolution is to make possible the development of a plan to take a different action in the future—to change the *doing* component of the total behavior. Thus, the problem-solving strategies of conflict resolution are action oriented, and a program of conflict resolution education is by definition a program of action strategies utilizing the four principles of conflict resolution to plan future behaviors.

A conflict resolution education program supplements the behavior management program in at least two ways: First, it provides opportunities and processes for individuals to choose to deal with conflicts in their early stages. Dealing with conflicts early may stop them from escalating to what is perceived as misbehavior within the system—the proactive, prevention capacity. Second, it provides a planning process to design acceptable behaviors that individuals may choose when misbehavior has occurred—the reality therapy planning capacity. Emotion abilities are likely prerequisite for each of the other foundation abilities. An individual without emotional self-control and without the capacity and courage to express emotions is unlikely to develop an orientation toward collaborative problem solving, to understand the differences between reality and perception, to be an effective communicator or generator of options, and to be able to control the emotional mind so the logical mind can critically appraise possibilities. The elements of emotional intelligence—knowing one's emotions, managing emotions, motivating oneself, recognizing emotions in others, and handling relationships—are vital to the successful employment of conflict resolution strategies.

In summary, then, authentic conflict resolution education programs provide more than opportunity to develop the foundation abilities of orientation, perception, emotion, communication, creative thinking, and critical thinking. Such programs offer training and practice in at least one of the processes of conflict resolution, incorporating the foundation abilities for the effective employment of the four conflict resolution principles. Conflict resolution, at best, is difficult. Success requires more than good intentions. Even those with well-developed foundation abilities need a structured process to resolve most conflicts constructively. Further, the structured process will work best when it seems natural—a condition that develops only through repeated, successful practice.

Endnotes

1. J. Filner and J. Zimmer, "Understanding Conflict Resolution: School Programs for Creative Cooperation," *Update on Law-Related Education* vol. 20 no. 2 (1996), 4–6.

2. F. Schrumpf, D. K. Crawford, and R. J. Bodine, *Peer Mediation: Conflict Resolution in Schools,* rev. ed. (Champaign, IL: Research Press, 1997), 24.

3. R. Fisher, W. Ury, and B. Patton, *Getting to Yes: Negotiating Agreements without Giving In* (New York: Penguin, 1991), 83.

4. Schrumpf et al., *Peer Mediation*, 25–26.

5. Fisher et al., *Getting to Yes*.

6. Fisher et al., *Getting to Yes*.

7. Fisher et al., *Getting to Yes*, 11.

8. Fisher et al., *Getting to Yes*.

9. Fisher et al., *Getting to Yes*, 22.

10. Fisher et al., *Getting to Yes*, 29.

11. Fisher et al., *Getting to Yes*, 32.

12. Fisher et al., *Getting to Yes*, 11.

13. Fisher et al., *Getting to Yes*, 57.

Facilitating Emotional Intelligence: Activities for Developing Teachable Abilities

These learning activities are designed to be used in sequence, but it is not necessary to complete a whole lesson at one time. Some of these activities may best involve two to four sessions. Also, these activities can be repeated as often as review is needed: It is quite likely different discussions will ensue at different times.

Basic Needs

Purpose

Students will learn that our behavior is chosen and that the choices we make are always what we believe is our best attempt to meet basic needs for belonging, power, freedom, and fun.

Materials

Handouts 1, 2, and 3
Index cards

Procedure

1. Refer students to Handout 1, "Basic Needs," and discuss. Emphasize that we are constantly striving to satisfy basic internal needs. We each have basic needs for belonging, power, freedom, and fun. Our behavior is the choices we make to satisfy those needs.

2. Discuss that we might think that people or situations cause us to act a certain way, but this is not true. We act the way we do because we are trying to meet our basic needs. In other words, our behavior is really caused by what is inside us, not by what is outside.

3. Refer students to Handout 2, "How We Meet Our Basic Needs." Discuss the idea that although we all share the same basic needs, the things each of us chooses to do to meet these needs are different. For example, everyone has a need for

power. However, Paul gets this need met by developing his music skills. Elizabeth gets this need met by being on the soccer team. Darrin gets this need met by being able to draw cartoon heroes; Cassandra by being very knowledgeable about computers.

4. In the group, have a general discussion to elaborate on the idea of differing choices to meet the same need. Briefly solicit ideas on the following:

• What are some of the things you do for fun? (For each idea advanced, ask for a show of hands to the probe "How many of you would consider that behavior fun?")

• What are some choices you would make to get your belonging need meet?

5. Give each student a few index cards. Instruct students to use a card and make a list of persons they consider to be important in their life. The list might include family members, friends, teammates, and so forth.

6. Refer students to Handout 3, "How I Meet My Basic Needs." Instruct students to think about some things that they choose to do with the people on their list. Ask them to draw or write those things in the heart shape on Handout 3.

7. Tell students that we all like to be important and feel good about ourselves. Say, "Inside the star shape on Handout 3, draw or write what you do when you feel important or what you do when you feel good about yourself."

8. Tell students that to be free, people have to be able to make choices and decide things for themselves. Say, "Inside the butterfly shape, draw or write things you freely choose to do or decisions you make for yourself."

9. Say, "Inside the happy-face shape, draw or write the things you enjoy doing or things you do for fun."

10. Allow the students time to list five to seven things in each shape on Handout 3.

11. In groups of four or five, have students discuss the examples they recorded and compare how they are alike and how they are different.

12. Summarize that although we all have the same basic needs, we have each learned different ways to satisfy those needs.

BELONGING

POWER

FREEDOM

FUN

> Understanding our behavior
> begins with identifying the origin of the
> behavior. Most all of our behavior is
> determined by our attempts to meet basic
> needs for belonging, power, freedom, or fun.

- Our BELONGING need is met by developing and maintaining relationships with others where we have the opportunity to love, share, and cooperate.

- Our POWER need is met by achieving, accomplishing, and being recognized and respected.

- Our FREEDOM need is met by making choices in our lives.

- Our FUN need is met by laughing and playing.

We are all born with the same basic needs. However, the things we each choose to do to meet these needs may be different from what others choose.

How I Meet My Basic Needs

Instructions: In each need shape, draw or write some things you do
to meet your basic needs.

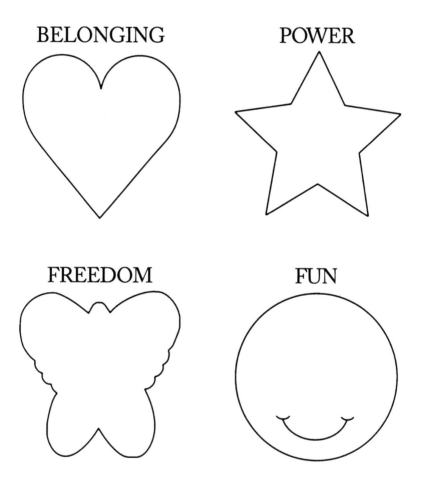

BELONGING

POWER

FREEDOM

FUN

Basic Needs and Conflict

Purpose

Students will learn that most conflicts between people involve attempts to meet basic needs for belonging, power, freedom, and fun.

Materials

Handouts 4, 5, and 6

Procedure

1. Reiterate that in Activity 1 we learned that although people all have the same basic needs, it is very likely that two people will choose different ways to satisfy those needs. Most every dispute between people involves the attempt to meet the basic needs of belonging, power, freedom, or fun.

2. Refer students to Handout 4, "Origins of Conflict," and discuss.

3. Refer students to Handout 5, "Looking at My Conflicts– Part 1." Ask students to record in each of the need shapes examples of conflicts with other young people they have experienced. Tell students that some of the conflicts might fit into more than one of the shapes.

4. Refer students to Handout 6, "Looking at My Conflicts– Part 2." Ask students to record in each of the need shapes examples of conflicts with adults they have experienced. Tell

students that some of the conflicts might fit into more than one of the shapes.

5. Have students in groups of four to five share what they recorded on Handout 5 and Handout 6. Instruct them to talk about each need and the conflicts they have experienced.

6. Discuss the ideas in the text boxes on Handout 5 and Handout 6. Solicit examples of experiences that might validate these statements.

Handout 4
Origins of Conflict

Understanding how to resolve a conflict begins with identifying the origin of the conflict. Most every dispute between people involves the attempt to meet the basic needs of:

- Belonging
- Power
- Freedom
- Fun

We might think that people or situations cause us to act a certain way, but this belief is not true. We act the way we do because we are trying to meet our basic needs. Here are some examples:

- Suppose you are upset because your friend is going to a birthday party and you were not invited. You might get into a conflict with the friend because you are not getting your need for *belonging* met.

- Suppose someone calls you a name and you get into an argument. Name calling shows a lack of respect, which is related to the *power* need.

- Suppose you are in a conflict with a parent about the chores you must do around the house. This conflict might be the result of your need to have the *freedom* to make your own choices about how to spend your time.

- You may be mad at the coach because you think you deserve more playing time, and her decision not to let you play is frustrating your *power* need—you think she doesn't recognize your ability, and that not playing deprives you of the chance to gain respect from your teammates and the fans.

- You may be upset with someone you want to spend time with because whenever you are with that person, you only do things that person wants to do. Your *freedom* need is not being met because you are not allowed to choose. You may not think the other person's choice is a fun thing to do and your *fun* need is not beginning met; however, just being with that person provides for your *belonging* need.

Others act they way they do because they are also trying to meet their basic needs.

We are all born with the same four basic needs. However, the things we each choose in order to meet those needs may be different from what others choose. These different choices may cause a conflict, either because two people are trying to satisfy the same basic need in two different ways or because they are each simulaneously trying to satisfy a different need.

Handout 5
Looking at My Conflicts—Part 1

Instructions: In each shape, draw or write examples of conflicts you
have experienced with other young people.

BELONGING POWER

FREEDOM FUN

Persons not directly involved in a conflict may become
aware of the conflict by observing the behavior of the
individuals who are involved. In social situations such as
school, when others become aware of our conflicts they
often see us as "acting up" or misbehaving rather than
simply choosing a way to meet our needs.

Looking at My Conflicts–Part 2

Instructions: In each shape, draw or write examples of conflicts you
have experienced with adults.

BELONGING

POWER

FREEDOM

FUN

When young people are in conflict with adults, the adults
may think that the young person has made a poor choice of
behavior to satisfy his or her basic needs. Often the adult
thinks that the young person is deliberately making a choice
that is designed to cause a problem to the adult. Other
times the adult may think the young person should have no
choice but should do whatever the adult wants.

Limited Resources Conflicts and Basic Needs

Purpose

Students will learn that conflicts that seem to be about shortages or limited resources are also about basic needs not being met.

Materials

Handout 7
Easel pad

Procedure

1. Explain that limited resources may appear to be the cause of some conflicts. Ask students to think of situations where conflicts resulted from not having enough of something—for example, not enough soft drinks for each person or not enough slices of pizza, not enough time with a friend or a special relative, not enough pieces of equipment on the playground or in the gym, not enough space for two kids in the front seat of the car by the window, and so on.

2. On the easel pad, create a list containing a variety of examples of conflicts that appear to involve a shortage of something.

3. Discuss how these conflicts usually get resolved:

   • Does an adult decide?

- Does the older person get what he or she wants?

- Does possession rule—the person who has, keeps?

- Is there a compromise?

- Do the people involved decide on a fair way to share?

4. Refer students to Handout 7, "Limited Resources and Conflict," and discuss the first four paragraphs.

5. Return to the list that was created on the easel pad and ask students to identify which basic needs were not getting met in each of the situations.

6. Discuss the text box of Handout 7. Ask students if they can think of examples when they were required to share and felt that it was not fair.

7. Summarize by telling students that limited resources usually do not totally define the problem and any solution that deals only with the limited resource will likely not be viewed as fair by at least one of the parties involved.

Handout 7
Limited Resources and Conflict

When *resources* are limited, conflicts may result. Conflicts that involve limited resources are about time, money, property, or some combination of these things. For example, two classmates might be having a conflict over property when they are arguing about who will get to use a certain book they both want for a report.

Think of examples of conflicts you have experienced involving limited resources:

- A conflict about *money*
- A conflict about personal/school *property*
- A conflict about *time*

We each want money or property or time because we see these as things that allow us to satisfy our basic needs. If we have money, we can afford to do more (freedom, fun, belonging). We can buy things like great clothes, sports equipment, or audio-video products to gain recognition (power).

When we have plenty of time, we can do our work (power) and also hang out with our friends (fun, belonging, freedom). When time is limited we may have to choose. Time conflicts usually involve not having enough time to do all we want to do, or there is a disagreement about what should be done when. Have you ever thought you had plenty of time to do your school work, your chores, and also talk to your friends, but an adult insisted you do the chores and the school work first?

> Unmet basic needs are at the heart of conflicts over limited resources. If the parties can communicate, they can develop a plan to cooperate and share the limited resources. Even though limited resources are at issue, it may be very difficult for the parties to cooperate unless they can see that doing so satisfies their basic needs.

Different Values Conflicts and Basic Needs

Purpose

Students will learn that conflicts that seem to be about differences between people are also about basic needs not being met.

Materials

Handouts 8 and 9
Easel pad

Procedure

1. Have students line up according to the following characteristics:
   First: Tallest to shortest
   Second: Darkest hair to lightest hair
   Third: Shortest hair to longest hair
   Fourth: Lightest skin to darkest skin

2. Discuss how it felt to be placed in a line based on physical characteristics. (Students may report feeling uncomfortable about being grouped in this way, especially with regard to skin color. However, their discomfort can help sensitize them to the importance of underlying differences.)

3. Explain that it is easy to see physical differences but that other differences are not so easy to see—for example, things we believe in, attitudes, or religious preferences.

4. Explain that some conflicts appear to be because the people involved are very different. These conflicts involve different values. Refer students to Handout 8, "Cultural and Social Diversity Worksheet" and instruct them to complete it.

5. Form discussion groups of four to six students per group. Ask students to use their completed worksheets to help them think of a time when they felt judged, teased, or discriminated against because of one or more of the gifts they have received. Have them share these experiences in their small groups. Allow three or four volunteers to share their experiences with the larger group.

6. Tell students that values may be expressed as racism, sexism, classism, ageism, and so forth; therefore, conflicts about different values may be the result of prejudice and discrimination. Conflicts involving prejudice and discrimination are very difficult to resolve. Often fear, anger, and/or mistrust are prevalent in these conflicts.

7. Refer students to Handout 9, "Different Values and Conflict," and discuss.

8. Ask students to think about some conflicts they have had because of differences between themselves and another person.

9. On the easel pad, create a list containing a variety of examples of conflicts that appear to involve different values. Ask students to identify which basic needs were probably not getting met in each of the situations.

10. Summarize that conflicts involving differences in values are also caused by basic needs not getting met. These conflicts are difficult for us because when values are different, people often perceive the conflict as a personal attack. The initial behaviors chosen in response to this type of conflict often make the problem bigger.

11. Emphasize that satisfying the basic psychological needs is what drives behavior and thus the basic needs are at the core of conflicts. The resolution of many conflicts will require that the disputants look beneath the surface issue—limited resources or different values—that appear to frame the conflict. Resolution will most likely involve new plans to satisfy the basic psychological needs for belonging, power, freedom, or fun for each of the participants.

Handout 8
Cultural and Social Diversity Worksheet

Each of us has a variety of gifts, making each of us unique. You probably like some gifts more than you like other gifts. You may even wish you could exchange some of your gifts: Some you can change, but many you cannot. Check the categories or fill in the blanks for those items that are most nearly true about you.

Gift of Race/Ethnicity

- ❏ African American
- ❏ Asian American
- ❏ European American
- ❏ Hispanic American
- ❏ Native American
- ❏ Other _____

Gift of Ability

- ❏ Artistic
- ❏ Leadership
- ❏ Mathematical
- ❏ Mechanical
- ❏ Musical
- ❏ Physical
- ❏ Verbal
- ❏ Other _____

Gift of Culture

Family practices in:
- ❏ Religion
- ❏ Dress
- ❏ Food
- ❏ Holidays
- ❏ Language
- ❏ Other _____

Gift of Gender

- ❏ Female
- ❏ Male

Different Values and Conflict

We all have different *values*. Values are the beliefs, convictions, priorities, and rules we follow. Differences in values may result in conflicts.

Conflicts involving values tend to be difficult to resolve because when people's values are different, they often perceive the dispute as a personal attack. When a person feels attacked, he or she often either withdraws or attacks—and neither of these reactions will likely deescalate the conflict. For example, a student who values honesty in her friends will probably be very upset and angry if she learns that a friend has lied to her.

Our values are very much influenced by who we are and by our social environment. Our gender, our race, our social status, our ethnic group, our culture, and our abilities are differences that all play a part in forming our values. These differences are referred to as *cultural diversity* and *social diversity*. They also include diversity of religion, national origin, age, sexual orientation, and so on.

Values are wants that we use to guide our actions because we believe that they show us the best way to satisfy our needs. We may believe this because of our gifts or because we think our gifts are better than or not as good as another's gifts.

> Unmet basic needs are at the heart of conflicts over different values.

The student who is angry because her friend lied to her is attempting to satisfy her belonging need, but she finds it difficult to share and cooperate with someone who is dishonest. Her friend may also be attempting to satisfy her belonging need, but she fears that if she is honest with her friend the truth will hurt her friend's feelings and the friend will become angry and choose to avoid her.

Resolving conflicts involving different values does not mean the disputants have to change or align their values. They may need to agree to disagree, respectfully. Often a mutual acknowledgment that they see things differently is the first step toward a resolution.

> Individuals in a conflict involving different values can plan a different, more acceptable behavior if they focus on the mutual satisfaction of basic needs.

Rights and Responsibilities

Purpose

Students will understand responsibility as a behavior and a right as a guaranteed condition and will understand the relationship between rights and responsibilities.

Materials

Handouts 10 and 11
Newsprint sheets (loose)
Markers
Masking tape
Easel pad

Procedure

1. Explain that the idea of responsibility is important to people who live and work together. "Your home is one place where you live and work with others for several hours each day. Each of you is from a different home."

2. Divide the class into groups of four or five. Give each group a few sheets of newsprint and some markers. Ask each group to discuss the chores and jobs they are expected to do at home. Have each group make a list of these chores or jobs.

3. Invite the groups to share their lists and post them in the room.

4. Explain that each chore or job that we are expected to do

regularly is a responsibility and that others must be able to trust that we will do our chores and jobs—that we will fulfill our responsibilities.

5. Ask the class to share ways they are expected to behave at home. Give examples, such as saying thank you or excuse me, cleaning up your own mess, showing respect for adults. Once the class has the idea, invite the small groups to create a second list of these expectations.

6. Ask the groups to share their lists; post them next to the chores and jobs lists for each group. Explain that the way we are always expected to behave is a *responsibility*.

7. Examine the posted lists and find some common at-home responsibilities for class members. Explain that although there are some similarities, there are also differences from home to home.

8. Refer students to Handout 10, "Rights and Responsibilities," and discuss the "responsibilities are" section.

9. Explain that school is another place where you live and work with others for several hours each day. "Unlike your different homes, each of you attends the same school."

10. Ask students to think of responsibilities they have at school. Refer them again to the "responsibilities are" statements from Handout 10. Compile a list of six to ten school responsibilities. Explain that, although there may be some slight differences in our responsibilities depending on our specific school activities, we all have the same general responsibilities at school.

11. Arrange a class in a class-meeting circle. Explain that the purpose of this class meeting is to understand what a right is.

12. Tell the class to think about the word *privilege* and think about the word *freedom*. Ask the class to give examples of privileges (for example, being allowed to play a computer game if other work is completed) or freedoms (for example, choosing your own friends) given to students during the school day.

13. On the easel pad, list the privileges and freedoms students generate. After several examples are recorded, ask:

    - What is a privilege?
    - What is a freedom?
    - How are they different or the same?

    Elicit the idea that freedoms and privileges are synonymous.

14. Tell the class that privileges or freedoms that are given to everyone all the time are called *rights*. Ask students to think of rights that they think students have in school. Compile students' ideas on the easel pad under the heading "Students Have the Right to . . ." Reduce the list to those items the group agrees should be rights for everyone, all the time.

15. Summarize by referring students to Handout 10. Call attention to the "rights are" section and explain that rights are guaranteed conditions; rights are what we should always expect.

16. Refer students to Handout 11, "Sample School Rights and Responsibilities." You may substitute your actual school rights and responsibilities list if one exists. Discuss the text box. Although rights are guaranteed conditions, in reality having rights in any social setting, such as at home or at school, is dependent upon our accepting our responsibilities but also on all others accepting their responsibilities.

Handout 10
Rights and Responsibilities

Responsibilities are ...

- Something you are always expected to do
- A way you are always expected to act
- A way you are expected to treat someone else

Rights are ...

- Guaranteed conditions (what you should always expect)

Sample School Rights and Responsibilities

Rights	Responsibilities
I have the right:	I have the responsibility:
To be treated with respect and kindness: No one will tease me, demean me, or insult me.	To treat all others with respect and kindness by not teasing, demeaning, or insulting them.
To be myself: No one will treat me unfairly due to looks, abilities, beliefs, or gender.	To honor individual differences by treating all others fairly regardless of looks, abilities, beliefs, or gender.
To be safe: No one will threaten me, bully me, or damage or remove my property.	To help make the environment safe by not acting dangerously, by securing my property, by not threatening or bullying others, and by respecting the property of others.
To be heard: No one will yell at me, and my opinions will be considered.	To listen to others, consider their opinions, and allow others to be heard.
To be free to express my feelings and opinions without criticism and to learn about myself through constructive feedback.	To express myself respectfully in ways others can hear me and to allow others to express themselves, and to provide others with constructive feedback.
To learn and to be provided assistance to do so.	To accept assistance when given in the spirit of increasing my opportunity to learn and grow and to unconditionally provide assistance to others whenever I can do so.
To expect that all rights will be mine in all circumstances and to receive assistance from those in charge when that is not the case.	To accept assistance when given in the spirit of increasing my opportunity to learn and grow and to unconditionally provide assistance to others whenever I can do so.

> Enjoying a right requires everyone to accept certain responsibilities.

Responsible Behavior and Basic Needs

Purpose

Students will learn that responsible behavior involves choices to satisfy one's basic needs without denying similar opportunities to others.

Materials

Handouts 4, 10, 11, and 12
Easel pad

Procedure

1. Review the definitions of responsibilities and rights from Handout 10 (p. 204). Review the text box from Handout 11 (p. 205).

2. Refer students to Handout 12 in this activity, "Responsible Behavior and Basic Needs," and discuss the top portion, including the first text box. Emphasize that in a social situation such as school, this vision of peace is achievable. To achieve the vision, each person must make peace his or her personal job—his or her responsibility.

3. Remind students that our behavior is determined by the choices we make and that those choices are actually our attempts to satisfy our basic needs for belonging, power, freedom, or fun. Discuss the next two statements on Handout 12.

4. Refer students to Handout 4 (pp. 189–190). Say, "Consider that you are the person in the first situation, in which you may get into a conflict with your friend because your friend is invited to a party and you are not. You believe your belonging need is not being met. What are choices you could make in this situation to satisfy your belonging need besides getting into a conflict with your friend?" List the possibilities on the easel pad. Continue to brainstorm ideas until you have five or more.

5. Repeat this process for each of the other scenarios on Handout 4.

6. Ask students to consider all of the possible choices generated for each scenario. Eliminate from consideration any possibility that would deny the individual the opportunity to get his or her need met. Instruct students not to seek what they think is "the best" way but to seek any idea that could satisfy the individual's need to some extent. Challenge each suggestion for elimination and eliminate only if there is broad consensus that the idea does not work.

7. Now consider the ideas remaining for each scenario. Eliminate any idea that will be unfair to someone else directly involved in the scenario or that will create an obvious problem for others even though they may not be directly involved. Several possible behavior choices for each scenario should be left.

8. Summarize by referring to the text box at the bottom of Handout 12. Emphasize that the socially responsible behavior may not be the first behavior that comes to mind, and it may also not be the easiest behavior. When we want to enjoy all our rights, we are obligated to choose socially responsible behavior.

- Peace is a *right*.
- Peace is a *responsibility*.

> *Peace* is that state in which each individual fully exercises his or her responsibilities to ensure that all individuals fully enjoy all rights.

- Each person's ultimate responsibility is to satisfy his or her basic needs for belonging, power, freedom, or fun.
- Several behavior choices usually exist to satisfy our needs.

> A socially responsible person chooses behaviors that will satisfy his or her basic needs but also allow others to satisfy their basic needs. A socially responsible person does not choose behaviors that violate another's rights.

Basic Needs and the Social Context

Purpose

Students will learn that whether a behavior choice for satisfying a basic need is a responsible choice is often dependent on the social context.

Materials

Handouts 12 and 13
Easel pad

Procedure:

1. Refer students to Handout 13 in this activity, "Satisfying Our Basic Needs: Why We Make the Choices We Make," and discuss.

2. Ask students to think about times when they felt lonely, rejected, or unloved. Ask for volunteers to share with the class examples of times they experienced these feelings.

3. Tell the students that probably everyone has experienced such feelings at one time or another. Using the process of brain-storming, generate a list of possible behaviors one could choose to try to end or lessen the pain associated with such a feeling. Create a list of possibilities on the easel pad. Ask students to think of specific choices. For example, instead of "do

something with someone," give ideas like "ask a classmate to sit with you at lunch" or "invite your mom to watch her favorite TV show with you in your bedroom."

4. When you have a sizeable list of possible choices, evaluate each choice by asking, "Could this choice help someone feel less lonely or rejected or unloved?" Tell students to think about whether each behavior will help. Remind them that helping may not be the same as totally eliminating the feeling of loneliness or rejection or being unloved—it may be a choice that makes things temporarily better or a choice that moves someone in a direction to overcome the feeling of loneliness or rejection or of being unloved. Circle those choices that the majority of the class think could help.

5. Using each of the circled choices, have the group discuss the following:

   • Is this a choice that could help at school?

   • If yes, are there times during the school day or circumstances when the behavior might work best?

   • Are there times or circumstances at school when the behavior might not work, when the behavior might get you in trouble?

   • Is this a choice that might work regardless of the people present?

6. Summarize the discussion by referring to the text box on Handout 13 and also review the second text box on Handout 12 (p. 208). Tell the students that a responsible person often must choose different behaviors in different situations.

7. Ask students to think about times when they felt inadequate, unappreciated, or put down. Ask for volunteers to share with the class examples of when they experienced these feelings.

8. Repeat Steps 3 through 6 for the power need.

9. Ask students to think about times they felt trapped or helpless. Ask for volunteers to share with the class examples of times they experienced these feelings.

10. Repeat Steps 3 through 6 for the freedom need.

Satisfying Our Basic Needs:
Why We Make the Choices We Make

Each of us has the same basic needs:

- Belonging
- Power
- Freedom
- Fun

Each of us has learned behavior choices to satisfy these needs. When a basic need is satisfied, we experience feelings that we associate with pleasure. We tend to continue to choose behaviors that have worked for us before; that is, those choices that give us pleasure.

When a basic need is not satisfied or is frustrated, we experience feelings that we associate with pain (unpleasantness).

- When the *belonging* need is frustrated, we may feel lonely or rejected or unloved.

- When the *power* need is frustrated, we may feel inadequate or unappreciated or put down.

- When the *freedom* need is frustrated, we may feel helpless or trapped.

- When the *fun* need is frustrated, we may feel lethargic or grumpy or stressed.

When we feel pain, we always behave in a way we think will cause the pain to go away or lessen. Whether our behavior choice works as well as we would like may depend on where we are or the people we are with.

Discussion Topics for Class Meetings

The following discussion topics for class meetings (see chapter 6) will reinforce and expand on the concepts presented in Activities 1 through 7.

1. What are all the socially responsible behaviors you can choose to satisfy the belonging need?

    - Which of those behaviors would be socially responsible in school?

    - When would those behaviors be socially responsible in school?

2. What are all the socially responsible behaviors you can choose to satisfy the power need?

    - Which of those behaviors would be socially responsible in school?

    - When would those behaviors be socially responsible in school?

3. What are all the socially responsible behaviors you can choose to satisfy the freedom need?

    - Which of those behaviors would be socially responsible in school?

    - When would those behaviors be socially responsible in school?

4. What are all the socially responsible behaviors you can choose to satisfy the fun need?

    - Which of those behaviors would be socially responsible in school?

- When would those behaviors be socially responsible in school?

5. What are some examples of a behavior choice that would be socially responsible in one setting but not in another? What are the settings?

6. What are some examples of behavior choices that were suggested for you by others but that you do not think would be need fulfilling for you?

7. Why do you think the behaviors suggested in the last question would not satisfy your needs?

About the Authors

Richard J. Bodine, *Program Director, National Center for Conflict Resolution Education,* holds an undergraduate degree in teaching of mathematics and chemistry and has taught in elementary, middle school, high school, and junior college. He has a master's degree in special education, specializing in gifted children, and an advanced certificate of education in administration from the University of Illinois at Urbana-Champaign. Previously a secondary school administrator and director of special regional education programs, he has consulted with numerous schools on gifted education, individualized learning programs, behavior management, and administrative issues, as well as directed teacher training institutes on innovative practice. In the past 6 years he has trained over 3,000 adults and over 1,300 youth in conflict resolution processes. He has taught graduate level courses in administration at the University of Illinois, including a course on principalship. For 20 years, he served as principal of Leal Elementary School in Urbana, Illinois. In 1992 he was the recipient of the Illinois State Board of Education "Those Who Excel" award as an outstanding administrator. He holds training certificates from CDR Associates of Boulder, Colorado, for Mediation, for Dispute Management Systems Design, and for Conflict Resolution in Organizations and is the coauthor of *Peer Mediation, The School for Quality Learning,* and *Creating the Peaceable School* (all published by Research Press); *Conflict Resolution Education: A Guide to Implementing Programs in Schools, Youth-Serving Organizations, and Community and Juvenile Justice Settings* (U. S. Department of Justice and U. S. Department of Education); and *The Handbook for Conflict Resolution Education* (Jossey-Bass).

Donna K. Crawford, *Executive Director, National Center for Conflict Resolution Education,* is a former public school educator, having taught in and served as principal of an early childhood center and as a district special education administrator with supervi-

215

sory responsibility for a regional program for students with emotional and behavioral disorders. She is an experienced mediator, reality therapist, and dispute resolution trainer. She holds a master's degree in special education and an advanced certificate of education in administration from the University of Illinois at Urbana-Champaign. Her background in alternative dispute resolution methods includes training from the Justice Center of Atlanta, the Illinois State Board of Education Department of Specialized Services, and the Harvard University Law School. She serves as a practicum supervisor for the Institute for Reality Therapy in Los Angeles and is certified in reality therapy. She has served on the National Association for Mediation in Education and the National Institute for Dispute Resolution joint committee to bring conflict resolution programs to colleges of education and is the coauthor of *Peer Mediation, The School for Quality Learning,* and *Creating the Peaceable School* (from Research Press); *Conflict Resolution Education: A Guide to Implementing Programs in Schools, Youth-Serving Organizations, and Community and Juvenile Justice Settings* (U. S. Department of Justice and U. S. Department of Education); and *The Handbook for Conflict Resolution Education* (Jossey-Bass).

405035